POLITICIDE

ARIEL SHARON'S WAR
AGAINST THE PALESTINIANS

BARUCH KIMMERLING

VERSO

London • New York

First published by Verso 2003
© Baruch Kimmerling 2003
All rights reserved

1 3 5 7 9 10 8 6 4 2

Verso
UK: 6 Meard Street, London W1F 0EG
USA: 180 Varick Street, New York, NY 10014–4606
www.versobooks.com

Verso is the imprint of New Left Books

ISBN 1–85984–517–7

British Library Cataloguing in Publication Data
Kimmerling, Baruch
    Politicide: Ariel Sharon's war against the Palestinians
    1. Sharon, Ariel, 1928–   2. Arab-Israeli conflict
    I. Title
    956.9'4054

    ISBN 1859845177

Library of Congress Cataloging-in-Publication Data
A catalog record for this book is available from the Library of Congress

Typeset in Perpetua by SetSystems, Saffron Walden, Essex
Printed in the USA by R.R. Donnelley & Sons
Printed in the UK by Bath Press

This book is dedicated to:

all the brave Israeli women who stand before Israeli checkpoints in the early morning hours to prevent soldiers from harassing Palestinian laborers seeking work in Israel;

the men and women from Israel and abroad who set up convoys bringing food and medicine to hungry Palestinian children in besieged towns, villages, and refugee camps;

and to the conscientious objectors who spent many months in military jail because they refused to participate in the criminal Lebanese War of 1982 or to commit war crimes in the recent Israeli–Palestinian War.

All of them express the genuine nature of Judaism and the true spirit and soul of Israel.

CONTENTS

PART II   THE ROAD TO SHARONISM

PART III   THE COMEBACK

INTRODUCTION

On February 6, 2001, Ariel Sharon won a direct election to become Prime Minister of Israel with an unprecedented 52 percent of the vote. This event marked both a turning point in the history of the country and the region and a basic change in the character of the Israeli Government and its political culture. This change was consolidated in a general election held on January 28, 2003, in which the rightwing bloc headed by Sharon won 69 out of 120 Knesset seats, and Sharon was re-elected Prime Minister of Israel. Sharon's landslide victory was made more impressive by the fact that he became the first Israeli Prime Minister to be re-elected for a second term since Menachem Begin in 1981.

Israel under Ariel Sharon became an agent of destruction, not only for its surrounding environment, but for itself as well, because its domestic and foreign policy is largely oriented toward one major goal: the politicide of the Palestinian people. By *politicide* I mean a process that has, as its ultimate goal, the dissolution of the Palestinian people's existence as a legitimate social, political, and economic entity. This process may also but not necessarily include their partial or complete ethnic cleansing from the territory known as the Land of Israel. This policy will inevitably rot the internal fabric of Israeli society and undermine the moral foundation of the Jewish state in the Middle East. From this perspective, the result will be a double politicide—that of the Palestinian entity and, in the long run, that of the Jewish entity as well. Therefore, the current Israeli Government poses a considerable danger to the stability and the very survival of all the peoples of the entire region.

Politicide is a process that covers a wide range of social, political, and military activities whose goal is to destroy the political and national existence of a whole community of people and thus deny it the possibility of self-determination. Murders, localized massacres, the elimination of leadership and elite groups, the physical destruction of public institutions and infrastructure, land colonization, starvation, social and political isolation, re-education, and partial ethnic cleansing are the major tools used to achieve this goal.

The politicide of the Palestinian people did not begin with Ariel Sharon's election. Rather, it is a consequence of the 1967 War and, partially, of the very nature and roots of the Zionist movement, and has been supported and reinforced by a series of regional and global events and processes.

The doomsday scenario that lies ahead has never been inevitable, and nor are the stages leading to it irreversible. However, Sharon's election and re-election, the circumstances that made them possible, and the internal political situation created in their aftermath have made this frightening vision more probable than it has ever been since 1948.

Israel never was a perfect liberal democracy, because the circumstances of its birth and its roots never allowed it to be. In spite of this, it was, with some measure of justification, considered by its Jewish population and the Western world as the only democracy in the Middle East. Indeed it was democratic in comparison to other regimes in the region. Israel was proud of its regular free elections, which provided its citizens with the opportunity to change the government and ruling elite according to their will. Israelis enjoyed relative freedom of expression—although this freedom existed in greater measure for Jews than for Arabs—as well as many other rights and liberties guaranteed by the law or the local political culture, and a judicial system that tried to provide a system of checks and balances, thus limiting the power of the bureaucracy and executive branches. Israel also tried to develop a limited welfare state. Today, these positive features are deteriorating as Israel becomes a Thatcherist and semi-fascist regime.

A mixture of elements characterizes the Israeli fascist tendencies:

- There is a drastic reduction in freedom of expression and a growing tendency to label opposition to the present policy as "treason." In fact, parliamentary opposition has been nearly liquidated by the previous creation of a Likud–Labor National Unity Government and by the refusal of Meretz, the only major Jewish-liberal-leftist party outside the government, to advocate alternative policies. Meretz, under the leadership of veteran Laborite Yossi Sarid, has preferred to remain inside the holy national consensus rather than perform the role of a real opposition party during a period of crisis by working to change this consensus. Labor's departure from the unity government did not make any difference since the damage was already done to Israeli society as well as to the party itself.

- The military are increasingly involved in political affairs and the media. Israel always was a militarized society and the boundaries between the military and political spheres were blurred. Officers of high and even middle rank have enormous influence in most aspects of Israeli society and political culture. Officers who left the military, usually when they were in their forties, were always considered self-evidently qualified for any civilian leadership position. Thus, the Israeli military has never needed to stage a coup-d'état to rule Israel, because the military—wielding varying degrees of power—has always been a partner in the major decision-making processes of a country which has consistently acted as though it were under siege and facing an existential crisis, regardless of whether the threat was real or not.

- Army personnel and former security officers, who are sometimes camouflaged as academic experts, have become the predominant interpreters of the situation in the mass media. Relations with the Palestinians are managed directly by consultations between the PM and the highest-ranking generals. Many of them, like the recently appointed Commander-in-Chief Moshe Ya'alon, are even more extreme in their daily operations than Sharon himself. The rest of the civilian ministers and parliamentary committees are informed only partially and after the fact about political developments, even though they are ideologically close to Sharon's views and have a tacit agreement with him on political goals.

- Sharon considers very few colleagues trustworthy. His authoritarian and suspicious personality, the decay of Israeli civil society, and the weakness of other political institutions have had undesirable effects. An informal regime has been created in which major decisions in a wide variety of spheres are taken by a single man, Ariel Sharon. Many former Israeli prime ministers—beginning with David Ben-Gurion—had a highly authoritarian style of decision-making; however, Sharon has succeeded in transforming a personal characteristic into an institutionalized system of rule and has successfully neutralized and marginalized any Jewish opposition.

- The most crucial element in Israel's recent drift toward fascism is the definition of "the other" (in this case the Palestinians of the West Bank and Gaza Strip, and even the Arab citizens of Israel, collectively) as a danger to the very existence of Israel as a nation and every Israeli individually. This definition prepares Israeli, Jewish, and world public opinion for drastic measures against the Palestinians. What before Sharon was considered unthinkable, or at least politically incorrect, has now become an explicit and respectable issue in mainstream Israeli political discourse—ethnic cleansing as a legitimate solution to the "demographic problem" of there being an Arab majority or approximate majority on the land. It is, however, unclear whether Israeli decision makers consider ethnic cleansing a real option or just a psychological warfare tactic that is being used as part of the process of politicide.

While the state nurtures public enmity against Arabs, it neglects the sharp increase in Israeli poverty. The total number of people living below the poverty level at the end of 2001 stood at 1,169,000—including over half a million children. The rate of unemployment rose from 8.8 percent in 2000 to 11 percent in 2001 and 12 percent in 2002. During the first two years of the second, al-Aqsa, Intifada, which started on September 29, 2000, the Israeli economy lost approximately $7 billion. The cost to the gross domestic product for the first year was 2.5 percent and for the second year 4.5 percent, and during these two years the military expenditure has been increased by $0.8 billion. In 2001 there was a negative growth in GNP of 1 percent and in 2002 of 1.5, a phenomenon unknown since the 1953 recession. While the poverty level, the highest since the 1950s, continues to increase, the state has remained indifferent to this process, leaving the fate of its impoverished citizens in the hands of a few charitable organizations. As the economic situation continues to deteriorate, Israeli citizens demand more activities against the "other"—the Arabs. The interactions among these processes create the main manifestations and local flavor of Israeli fascism. The major aims of the present book are to present and analyze these different background factors and examine how and why the Israeli state and its Jewish society have reached this abyss while most Israeli Jews remain unaware of the direction in which their society is headed.

Finally, a personal note: as an Israeli patriot, highly committed to the fate and well-being of Israel, my only country, and as a sociologist who has dedicated most of his professional life to studying Israeli and Palestinian societies, I am writing this book—in my temporary refuge in Toronto—with great sorrow and pain. My only personal objective for publishing this book is not "Israel bashing" by a "self-hating Jew," as most of my political and ideological opponents will argue—and as they claimed about some of my previous writings when they did not have better arguments—but to make a further attempt to open the eyes of a benevolent and humanistic people who do not yet see the real dangers besetting Israel. Indeed, the battle over the soul, fate, and well-being of Israel and all its citizens, Jews and Arabs, is global—as are most of the "local" issues of our era.

Toronto,
March 2003

PART I

PRESENT PAST

1 Internal Contradictions and Crisis

Following the 1967 War, the Israeli state and society became entangled in an ongoing and deepening existential crisis. This crisis was caused by basic internal contradictions that accompanied the gradual and selective absorption of the occupied Palestinian territories and population into the state. This absorption created an unprecedented economic boom and increased social mobility that obscured the crisis and become a part of it. By opening the borders of the West Bank and Gaza Strip, the Israeli labor market was flooded by cheap labor, the Palestinian market was opened up for the internal-export of Israeli products, and Palestinian lands became the target of Jewish colonization.[1]

---

1 Daily or weekly commuter laborers are the cheapest labor in any political-economic system. Living several miles from their potential workplaces, they travel to their jobs in the early morning and return home at night. They don't need housing and, since they are not citizens with civil rights, they don't receive social security,

This unusually convenient situation was accompanied by billions of dollars of American and other foreign aid that made the Israeli state one of the most prosperous in the world. All sectors of Israeli society, including the Arab citizens, enjoyed this prosperity. The situation also triggered a total restructuring of the economy and the social system. Most Israeli Jews left unskilled and semi-skilled occupations (in construction, services, agriculture, and low-tech industries), which were then filled by Palestinian workers, and moved to highly skilled (frequently high-tech) managerial and bureaucratic occupations. The number of Israeli companies listed on the NASDAQ stock market was second only to the number of American companies. The annual per capita production was, until the year 2000, one of the highest in the world and approached $18,000.

However, this prosperity was dependent on the continuing "good behavior" and endless cooperation of the Palestinian inhabitants of the West Bank and Gaza Strip, and their willingness to accept the Israeli policy of fully including them in the Israeli economy but completely excluding them from other spheres of the Israeli state. In fact, for nearly a whole generation the Palestinians accepted these colonial rules, benefiting from relative economic prosperity while enduring a complete deprivation of most human and civil rights as well as a total lack of any satisfaction deriving from self-determination, collective symbols, and the exercise of any ethnic and national identity. In fact, both societies became addicted to this deeply asymmetric situation

---

health insurance, or significant social services. In addition, the competition among them lowers their wages even more. It is a kind of modern slavery, and is more profitable and convenient for the host system than conventional international migrant workers.

and grew interdependent.[2] Most Israelis and Palestinians who grew up in this anomalous situation see it as natural and find it hard to imagine other kinds of relationship. This system started to crack only after the first Palestinian uprising began on December 9, 1987, and was completely crushed when the second uprising started. It is interesting to note that the Oslo Accords perpetuated the economic situation while pacifying the Palestinian population by granting them the satisfaction of symbolic self-determination. After the first Intifada began, the Israeli political economy adapted by importing foreign guest workers. Even though these workers did not threaten public safety, as Palestinian workers were perceived to do, they were more expensive and, since they were more permanent than Palestinian laborers who lived outside of Israel proper, they were viewed as a possible threat to the demographic composition of the society.[3]

Quite apart from the economic interest in the territories, a new complication arose after the 1967 War—the desire of Israeli society as whole, both left and right, to annex the historic heartland of the

2 This was probably why the occupied populations of the West Bank and Gaza Strip ignored the repeated calls to revolt that were issued by PLO leaders outside the territories. Instead they developed an alternative strategy of steadfastness (*samed*) on the land in order to avoid a second ethnic cleansing.

3 Sharon knows personally the value of cheap labor because he is the owner of what may be the largest private farm in Israel, the well-known Shikmim (Sycamores) Farm. The farm was bought in late 1972 with two generous loans granted by two American friends (Meshulam Riklis and Samuel Sax). When Sharon served as Minister of Agriculture and later Minister of Infrastructures, the ownership created some conflict of interests, which he solved by renting the farm to a friend. Sharon also owns a home in Arab East Jerusalem in order to demonstrate Jewish presence and to irritate the Arabs. He has never lived there but the home is heavily guarded by the border police.

Jewish people in the West Bank without annexing its Arab residents. A formal annexation would mean that Israel would no longer have a Jewish majority. Demographic changes would destroy the Jewish character of the state even if the Palestinians were not granted full citizenship. Political and demographic considerations collided with economic considerations and both contradicted the Kantian moral imperative as well as the Jewish Sage Hillel's demand not to do to the "other" what you don't wish the other to do you. This triple contradiction created a built-in crisis, leaving the Israeli state and society unable to make the important political decisions that were necessary to resolve the conflict. As time passed, the crisis became more explicit and the contradictory interests became aligned with political parties and were absorbed into personal and group identities and even into various religious streams ("hawks vs. doves," "right vs. left," or "Zionists vs. post-Zionists").

In 1977, when the rightwing nationalist bloc headed by the Likud Party came to power, its very first act was expected to be an immediate annexation of the entire West Bank (often called by the Biblical names, Judea and Samaria) and the Gaza Strip, which are regarded as part of the Land of Israel. After all, this was the main plank in the party's platform and what Menachem Begin, the party's leader, had advocated when he was in opposition. Annexation of the territories was also the reason Ariel Sharon, promptly after leaving the military in 1973, urged some medium and small rightwing and centrist parties to unite behind the veteran revisionist leader of Herut, which, until then, had been regarded as an eternal opposition party rather than a governing party.

The pretext for ignoring this part of the party platform was provided by Moshe Dayan, the prestigious Labor party figure, who deserted to the rival party and accepted an appointment as Foreign Minister in the new government on the condition that it avoid unilateral annexation. However, the real reason for the failure to annex the Palestinian occupied territories, which were perceived as the motherland of the Jewish people, was the existence of a rapidly growing Arab-Palestinian population in the occupied territories. This population, together with the Arab citizens of Israel, would at once transform the Jewish state into a bi-national entity even if the annexed population were not granted the rights of full citizenship and access to social welfare programs. Today, in spite of the unprecedented immigration of more than one million non-Arabs (Jews and non-Jews) from the former Soviet Union, the territory between the Mediterranean and the Jordan River contains about 5 million Jews (and non-Arabs) and 4.5 million Palestinians (citizens and non-citizens).

Current demographic projections indicate that future population figures will favor the Palestinians and further imperil the slender Jewish demographic majority. Arnon Sofer, a geographer from Haifa University, calculates that by the year 2020, a total of 15.1 million persons will live on the land of historic Palestine with Jews being a minority of 6.5 million. Moreover, even within Israel itself, in about twenty years the Jewish population will be reduced from its current 81 percent majority to a projected majority of barely 65 percent. Demographer Sergio della-Pergola of Hebrew University presented the same demographic picture and recommended that Israeli areas densely populated with Arabs be transferred to a Palestinian state in exchange for three major Jewish settlement blocs situated in the occupied Palestinian territories.

Two deeply rooted existential anxieties exist within the Jewish Israeli political culture: one concerns the physical annihilation of the state, an issue that is frequently used, abused and emotionally manipulated by many Israeli politicians and intellectuals, and the other the loss of the fragile Jewish demographic majority on which the supremacy and identity of the state rest. In fact, the loss of that demographic majority could be a prelude to politicide and the physical elimination of the state. Thus, the annexationist camp found itself in an impossible situation: one patriotic imperative, to possess the sacred land, contradicted the other patriotic imperative, to ensure a massive Jewish majority on the land. This internal contradiction caused some ridiculous suggestions, such as Moshe Dayan's proposal for a "functional division" of rule between Israel and Jordan. The core of the plan was that Israel should control the land militarily (for "security" reasons) and for settlement purposes, and Jordan should control the population politically and administratively, running all the services and granting the population full citizenship rights, including the right to vote for and be elected to the Jordanian parliament.[4] Obviously, neither the Jordanians nor the Palestinians were interested in such arrangements. It is important to note that Ariel Sharon held a more radical version of Moshe Dayan's plan that will be described later.

It must be said that only a minority of Jewish Israelis and even

---

4 In fact, this was the de facto situation for about ten years. The Hashemites were interested in controlling the population of the occupied territories in order to prevent the re-emergence of a strong Palestinian political identity and, following a tacit agreement with Israel, continued to pay the salaries of civil servants on the West Bank, including policemen, and to run the public educational system. However, Jordan had no interest in letting Israel control the land and water of the West Bank.

fewer Jews in the Diaspora had any moral qualms about depriving millions of Palestinian Arabs of all civil rights and most human rights. When philosopher and theologian Yeshayahu Leibowitz, one of Israel's leading moral voices, expressed his opposition, his argument was a selfish but correct one—that the occupation corrupted the occupiers and rotted the fabric of Israeli society. Significantly, he did not argue that the occupation was inherently evil. In fact, many of those who opposed the colonization of the occupied territories did it on practical terms, arguing that it tarnished the image of Israel and undermined its legitimate existence in the region. These considerations are completely correct but must be complemented by a moral imperative which unequivocally states that occupying and subjugating a people, unnecessarily colonizing them, and robbing them of land and water are profound sins.

Surprisingly, the elite of the annexationist camp is concerned not only with the continuity of the "Jewish character" of the state, but also with the long-term internal consequences of dominating another people. However, the solution contemplated by this camp is drastically different than withdrawal from the occupied territories and granting full citizenship rights to the Palestinian population of Israel. A large portion of the electorate that voted for Ariel Sharon expected him to provide the "proper solution" for the problems and internal contradictions of the right wing, but cared little about what kind of solution it would be. Sharon knows this very well, and, as will be demonstrated in this book, he may, from his supporters' point of view, be the right person in the right place at the right time.

2   Historical Context

The tragedy of Zionism was in its anachronism, but this could be observed only retrospectively. Following the Eastern European pogroms of 1880–1881, great waves of Jews emigrated to new host countries in search of a better and more secure life. Some arrived in the Holy Land, the traditional Jewish home and the object of their messianic dreams. However, the vast majority of Jews—even after immigration into the Holy Land was redefined politically and nationally by Zionism in European terms—preferred personal salvation by moving westward instead of the collective salvation suggested by Zionist ideology.

Thus, among the 65 million Europeans who migrated to the New World during the nineteenth century there were more than 4 million Jews, constituting 6 percent of all immigrants, compared with their 1.5 percent representation in the total population of Europe. During the first quarter of the twentieth century, about 20 percent of European Jewry emigrated to the Americas and only a handful to Zion. Were it not for the economic depression that began in the late 1920s and the subsequent immigration restrictions, it is highly probable that most European Jews would have emigrated to America in the 1930s, thus reducing the scope of the Holocaust and possibly preventing the establishment of the Jewish state in Palestine. But history does not recognize ifs.

For the local Arab population the "return" of the Jews, who thought they owned the country after two thousand years of exile, sounded ridiculous, unacceptable, and dangerous. To them, most of whom had inhabited the country for many generations, the Jews were European colonizers who tried to settle an Arab land and expropriate it under the protection of the imperial powers. Their suspicions were confirmed in 1917 when Britain took the land from the Muslim Ottoman Empire and granted it, via the Balfour Declaration, to the Jews in order to create a Jewish "national home" (namely a state). The Arab national institutions in Palestine were promptly formed and, from that time until 1993, consistently and firmly refused to accept any Jewish moral and political right over the country.

In the West, the reaction to Zionism and the Balfour Declaration was largely sympathetic. The Judeo-Protestant culture saw the return of the Jews to Zion as a theological premise and promise, which, over the decades, has been gradually expanded and politicized until it has reached its peak among present-day American fundamentalist Christians. The Arabs, apart from the romanticized noble-savage Bedouins, were dismissed as a primitive people unfit for self-determination. In the thirty years of British colonial rule (or the so-called Mandate), the Jewish ethnic community in Palestine developed into a viable immigrant-settler society that was transformed into the State of Israel in 1948

Immigrant-settler societies develop different policies toward the local population. In North America, Australia, and New Zealand, the free-frontier mentality completely ignored the existence of the local population as human beings and categorized them as part of the hostile natural environment, an attitude that ended with their genocide. In Afrikaner South Africa and Rhodesia, the local population was used as a cheap labor force but severely segregated from the white ruling race. In Catholic Latin America, the conquerors adopted an inverse strategy. After the annihilation and politicide of the great local cultures or civilizations (like the Aztec or Inca) and mass conversions to Christianity by the bulk of the surviving local population, the conquerors ideologically encouraged mixed marriages, albeit in different degrees. This inclusionary strategy created racially mixed and completely new nations.

In Palestine, both communities were highly exclusionary but were economically interdependent to varying degrees. The Jews were partially dependent on Arab labor and completely dependent on Arab land owners from whom they purchased property. Part of the Arab population enjoyed the capital influx that accompanied the different waves of Jewish immigration. Until 1948, neither the Jews nor the Arabs possessed enough political and military strength to get rid of the other, despite the great enmity among them that led to periodic violent clashes culminating in the great Arab-Palestinian revolt of 1936–1939.

It is crucial to understand that the Jewish community in Palestine was institutionally, cognitively, and emotionally built within an exclusive Jewish "bubble." The plans for the new state were similarly exclusive. The Jewish state was supposed to be purely Jewish and no political and bureaucratic tools were prepared for the possibility, mentioned in all partition proposals, that large Arab minorities would remain within the boundaries of the Jewish state. This possibility was only acknowledged in the rhetoric of the declaration of independence.

3   Precedents: The First Attempt at Politicide

The colonization of the West Bank and Gaza Strip by Jewish settlers led the Israeli state into a dead end. It is impossible to understand the intentions of Sharon and his political allies or their supposed solutions to this impasse without a knowledge of what happened during the inter-ethnic war of 1948. The "miracle" of 1948 refers to the fact that the Jewish state's territories were enlarged far beyond the borders allocated to it by the United Nations resolution of November 29, 1947. But even more important, from the Israeli point of view, is that the territories were almost completely cleared of their Arab inhabitants and that the rival Arab-Palestinian community ceased to exist as a socio-political entity.

The historian Benny Morris demonstrated in two different volumes (*The Birth of the Palestinian Refugee Problem* and *Righteous Victims: A History of Zionist-Arab Conflict*) how deeply rooted the idea of population "transfer" was in mainstream Zionist thinking, but he failed to make a connection between these ideas and the actual events of the 1948 War. The full story of that ethnic cleansing was told in the eight-volume *Book of Haganah History*, an official publication of the Israeli military publishing house. This Hebrew series has never been translated into any foreign language.

According to this publication, the first military doctrine that can be considered an Israeli military doctrine was the so-called Plan D (*Tochnit Daleth*). It was developed by General Yigael Yadin, the head of the operations branch of the Israeli armed forces (officially established on May 31, 1948), and launched on March 10, 1948, in anticipation of the expected military clashes between the state-making Jewish community and the Arab community and the assumed intervention by military forces of Arab states. In the plan's preamble, Yadin stated that

> [The] aim of this plan is the control of the area of the Jewish State and the defense of its borders [as determined by the UN Partition Plan] and the clusters of [Jewish] settlements outside the boundaries [allocated by the UN to the Jewish state], against regular and irregular enemy forces operating from bases outside and inside the [Jewish] state.

Furthermore, the plan suggested the following actions, among others, in order to reach these goals:

> [Actions] against enemy settlements located in our, or near our, defense systems [i.e., Jewish settlements and localities] with the aim of preventing their use as bases for active [hostile] armed forces. These actions should be executed as following: destruction of villages by fire, explosives, and mining—especially of those villages over which we cannot gain [permanent] control. The gaining of control will be accomplished in accordance with the following methods: encircling the village and searching it, and in the event of resistance destroying the resisting forces and expelling the population beyond the boundaries of the State.

As in many other cases, what seems at first glance a limited and purely military doctrine, that prepared the field for a possible invasion of Arab armies, in fact comprised far-reaching measures that would lead to a complete demographic, ethnic, social, and political transformation of Palestine from an Arab land to a Jewish state. Plan D was not like so many military plans which were formulated by a general staff and then left on the shelf. It was actually implemented. On May 14, 1948, State (of Emergency) D was declared and all combatant units received orders to execute Plan D.

Implementing the order and holding to the spirit of this doctrine, the Jewish military forces conquered about 20,000 square kilometers of territory (compared with the 14,000 square kilometers granted them by the UN Partition Resolution) and cleansed them almost completely of their Arab inhabitants. About 750,000 Arabs who lived on the land before it fell under Jewish control became refugees following the 1948 War. Fewer than 100,000 Arabs remained under Jewish control after the conclusion of ceasefire agreements with the Arab states who had invaded the country in order to help their Palestinian brothers prevent the establishment of the Jewish state, or simply to share the loot. An additional 50,000 were included within the Israeli state's territory following the Israeli–Jordanian armistice agreements that transferred several Arab villages to Israeli rule. From this point of view, the doctrine established by Plan D closely fitted both the requirements of the inter-communal war and the subsequent stage of inter-state war, after the internal-communal enemy was eliminated.[5]

5 In fact, the armies of the Arab states were using the outdated doctrine that advancing military troops must conquer and destroy any settlement or resisting forces in order to avoid leaving their rear lines and flanks unguarded. Had they used the alternative doctrine of a speedy advance toward the enemy's large population centers and main concentrations of troops, they probably would have achieved a completely different outcome in the 1948 War.

More than that, the doctrine clearly reflected the local Zionist ideological aspirations to acquire a maximal Jewish territorial continuum, cleansed from an Arab presence, as a necessary condition for establishing an exclusive Jewish nation-state. Until the 1948 War, Jewish public agencies and private investors succeeded in buying only about 7 percent of the land of Palestine, which proved to be enough to build a viable community but exhausted their financial abilities and failed to provide land reserves for the expansion of Jewish Palestine. Now, they decided to use the sword instead of money to considerably enlarge their territorial resources. The British colonial regime provided a political and military umbrella under which the Zionist enterprise was able to develop its basic institutional, economic, and social framework, but it also secured the essential interests of the Arab collectivity. When the British umbrella was removed, the Arab and the Jewish communities found themselves face-to-face in what seemed like a zero-sum situation. By rejecting the partition plan, the Arab community and its leadership were confident not only in their absolute right to control the whole country, but also in their ability to do so. The Jewish community's leadership knew that they did not have enough power to control the entire territory of Palestine and to expel or to rule its Arab majority so they accepted the partition plan but invested all their efforts in improving its terms and maximally expanding their boundaries while including as small an Arab population as possible within them.

There is no hard evidence that, despite its far-reaching political consequences and meanings, Plan D was ever officially adopted at the political level, or even discussed in that way. Were I to adopt a soft conspiracy-theory approach, I might conclude that many national leaders knew very well that there were orders and plans that were better not discussed or presented officially. In any case, the way the Jewish military operations of 1948 were conducted leaves no doubt about the fact that this was indeed the doctrine used by the Jewish military forces during the War, or about the spirit and perceptions behind it.

Most of Israel's non-combatant population, and even soldiers implementing the ethnic-cleansing policy, were not necessarily aware of the consequences of their deeds, possessing only the local and fragmented picture of the battlefield as a cleansing field. Several years after the war, Israel's greatest novelist, Yizhar Smilansky, wrote a short story entitled "Chirbet Hizza." The story described the feelings of a sensitive young Israeli soldier who executed the order to put the inhabitants of an entire Arab village on a truck and deport them beyond the border. Smilansky described the internal conflicts and moral hesitations of his young character and his shame over the uprooted people. Smilansky did not avoid hinting about the similarities between the evacuation of Arabs and the evacuation of Jews by Nazis in Europe. On the other hand, the young soldier happily imagined the beautiful Jewish kibbutz that would be established on the confiscated land. Smilansky also depicted his character, the only soldier in the unit that had moral hesitations about executing the order, as being the object of mockery by others in his unit.

Thus, during the first stage of the 1948 War, the Jewish community was able to carry out an almost complete ethnic cleansing of the rival community, a process which was, at that time, accepted by most of the international community as a natural consequence of that war. This was a total war, and if the Arabs won, they were expected to annihilate the Jews of Palestine, and not just commit politicide. When viewed in this context, the reasons for this consequence of the war become self-evident. Additionally, all this happened just three years after the terrible Nazi genocide against the Jewish people and at a time when millions of refugees and displaced people still wandered through Europe following the ravages of the Second World War. To this day, many Palestinians argue that they have paid the major price for European crimes against the Jewish people.

A less well-known and well-documented precedent occurred during the last two days of what is arrogantly called the Six Day War. After Israel decisively defeated the Egyptian and Jordanian armies as well as the Syrian air force (the air forces of most of the surrounding Arab states were destroyed on the ground by a successful and well-prepared surprise attack by the Israeli air force), a powerful lobby of the northern kibbutzim demanded that the government and general staff take over the Syrian Heights, lately renamed the Golan Heights. For years, these settlements suffered from heavy Syrian artillery bombardments—some of them following Sharon's provocations when he commanded a brigade on the Northern Front—and from the continuous military quarrels between Israel and Syria over the sources of the Jordan River. Now, the settlements saw a unique chance to escape the Syrian threat and to take revenge, but above all they lusted for the fertile land and abundant water of the territory. After two days of bloody battles, Israel conquered the territory (including the city closest to Damascus, Qunetra, which has been returned to Syria) and expelled about 80,000 Syrian Arab peasants before completely leveling almost 130 villages. Only the Druze villages remained intact, following the intervention of the Israeli Druzes, who were considered strong allies of Israel and are the only non-Jewish ethnic group, except for the small Circassian community, who are conscripted into the Israeli armed forces. In 1982 this territory was annexed to Israel and settled, while East Jerusalem was annexed immediately after the 1967 War and became part of the "reunified city."

Today, some of Israel's more chauvinistic leaders and public figures have explicitly adopted the idea of an ethnic-cleansing policy, waiting only for the proper time to implement it, while most of the other rightwing politicians, including Sharon, remain silent and never express moral reservations about it.[6] A notable exception is Benjamin Z. Begin, the son of the late Menachem Begin. Quite interestingly, until the beginning of this century, the very occurrence of the 1948 ethnic cleansing was firmly rejected and denied by Israeli leaders, intellectuals, and even historians—except for a handful of dissident historians and social scientists who were accused of falsifying Israeli historiography for reasons connected to their anti-Zionist inclinations, self-hatred, or search for personal fame. The official version of the "Arab flight" was that they fled because of their fear of internal

6 Some examples of these figures are Rehavam Zeevi, who was recently assassinated by a Palestinian elimination team; Rabbi Benny Elon, the current and former head of the Moledet Party; Avigdor Lieberman, the leader of one of the Russian parties; and Ephraim Eitam (Fein), the head of the important and respected National Religious Party. The names of many prominent national religious and Orthodox rabbis can also be added to this list. The original proponent of the forceful ethnic cleansing of all Arabs from the entire Land of Israel was Meir Kahane, whose Kach Party won one seat in the Knesset in 1984. In 1985, an amendment was passed forbidding avowedly racist candidates from running for the Knesset. To skirt this law, Kahane's followers adopted the code phrase "transfer by their own choice." However, since everyone knows that only a negligible minority of Arabs will choose to leave voluntarily, this new formulation is understood as mere lip-service to the anti-racism law.

instability (correct for a minority of upper- and middle-class Palestinian Arabs) and because leaders of Arab states called on them to leave the country in order to make room for invading Arab armies that would annihilate the Jewish entity (a completely false argument). Later, when Israel was asked to accept the return of the refugees, it refused, using the argument that an exchange of population and properties had been made: Israel "absorbed" the persecuted Jews from Arab lands, and the Arab states received in exchange their Palestinian brothers and the property of mainly Iraqi and Egyptian Jews.

Even if the cleansing committed in 1948 is now less frequently denied, it is not yet common knowledge in Israel. However, a core group of rightwing leaders and settlers perceive it not only as a precedent but as the first stage of an ongoing process. According to this view, the very survival of the state is in doubt unless Jewish lands are purified of Arabs as soon as possible. Today's ruling coalition includes parties that promote "transfer" of the Palestinian population as a solution to the "demographic problem." Politicians, including Knesset member Michael Kleiner and Benny Elon, the Minister of Transportation, are regularly quoted in the media as suggesting the forcible expulsion of Arabs from the country. In a recent interview in *Ha'aretz*, Chief of Staff Moshe Ya'alon described the Palestinians as a "cancerous manifestation" and equated the military actions in the occupied territories with "chemotherapy," suggesting that more radical treatment may be necessary. Prime Minister Sharon has backed this "assessment of reality." The escalating racist demagoguery concerning the Palestinian citizens of Israel may indicate the scope of the crimes that are possibly being considered, perhaps planned, and which wait only for the proper time for them to be implemented.

4 Ideology and Military Practices

The military, social, political, and global conditions that led in 1947 to the formulation of Yigael Yadin's military doctrine have changed considerably since March 1948, in part due to the successful implementation of Yadin's plan. However, some of the basic premises and ideological perceptions behind Plan D are still extant and deeply rooted in Israeli social and military thought and, more importantly, in the interaction between them. One of the most basic of these premises is the following: There is a concern that there exists a demographic asymmetry between the combatant sides—the Jews are always "the few" and the Arabs are always "the many." Yadin did not, however, explicitly acknowledge that his order for the destruction of hostile Arab villages over which the Jewish forces could not gain permanent control was rooted in the scarcity of manpower and in the inability to form a standing army to exercise direct control over the hostile Arab population that had fallen under Jewish rule. Most of the Muslim and some Christian Arab villages and neighborhoods were considered hostile by definition. Even some Arab populations defined as friendly were removed—as happened, for example, to the Maronite villages of Bir'm and Iqrit, or the Muslim downtown quarter of Haifa. The assumption of demographic asymmetry became the baseline for all further formulations of national security doctrines, including the recent one published in 1996 by General Israel Tal, based on the military, social, and political consequences of "the few against the many" presumption.

The immense demographic discrepancy between the Jewish settler-society and its Arab environment is perhaps the main factual and objective ingredient in the whole Israeli national security discourse. However, even in this case, the military strategist has a large degree of freedom to play with different boundaries of Jewish–Arab relations. These boundaries should be divided as follows: the Palestinian circle itself has at least three subdivisions—the Palestinian citizens of Israel, the Palestinians within the territories occupied after the 1967 War, and the Palestinians all over the world (or in the *gurba*, the Palestinian exile). Next are the Arab states that border Israel (Lebanon, Syria, Jordan, and Egypt). Arab states not bordering Israel (Iraq, Saudi Arabia, the Gulf States, Libya, etc.) are included in the next circle, and, when taken together with the bordering states, are sometimes referred to as the Arab World. When the conflict is perceived as religious warfare, the entire Muslim World (including Iran, Pakistan, and Indonesia) could be included. Before its collapse, the Soviet bloc was sometimes considered an integral part of the conflict but in this case the situation should have been regarded as a confrontation between superpowers. That perception still remains in the form of a vague outlook of "the West versus the rest," especially in the context of a supposed worldwide war against international terrorism, which has been overemphasized by George W. Bush following the September 11, 2001 catastrophe.

Additionally, some xenophobic Jewish subcultures adhere to a metaphysical perception of the cosmic order that regards the entire gentile world, or at least most of it, as being against the Jewish people. It is indicative that during the sixties and seventies one of the most popular Hebrew songs contained the words "the entire world is against us" (*ha'olam qulo negdenu*) and included the subtext that God will save "us," and that that is why the Jews are ultimately protected. Thus, even the most quantifiable, objective and factual ingredient— the quantity of the enemies—can be the subject of manipulation and social construction.

There has been a continuous stress on the importance of settlements as part of the state-building effort, as a part of the defense system, and primarily as a tool for determining the state's geographical, social, and political boundaries. A consequence of this view was a decision made in 1947 to defend all defensible settlements, even if they were located outside the borders of the territories allocated for the Jewish state. This military doctrine was complementary to the decision to destroy all 370 Arab localities which were perceived as endangering access to Jewish settlements, including those outside the 1947 partition plan boundaries, and to expel their inhabitants. Thus, while the political system in 1948 accepted the partition plan, the military system took a doctrinal decision that grossly altered its principles. This pattern of subjugating political decisions to quasi-military but in fact ideological needs was to be repeated many times in the future.

As is understandable from the above description, the macro-security doctrine adopted by the Jewish military system was, almost from the start, offensive in nature. Later, the offensive characteristics of the Israeli military doctrine were greatly expanded and elaborated. Some military experts added the so-called indirect approach, attributed to the British military expert and analyst B.H. Liddell Hart, to the offensive character of Israeli war-making practices. This approach calls for the concentration of massive forces, deception, a surprise attack against the enemy's unsuspected weak point through unconventional means, and then the immediate exploitation of the expected success. The Israeli political scientist and military analyst Dan Horowitz added to this strategy an additional dimension of "flexible responsiveness." Horowitz depicted the highly mobile battlefield as a chaotic situation, in which the supposed chains of command and communication no longer exist. In such a situation, the small isolated unit must operate on its own initiative, guessing what the general command expects from it. Horowitz stated that he attributed to the Israeli soldier the quality of flexibility, because of the Israeli way of socialization, while the Arab soldier lacked this and thus was usually highly dependent on the ordinary chain of command. This is a sophisticated example of the mythologizing of the Israeli military and its society, a widespread phenomenon between 1956 and 1973 employed to glorify and sanitize Israel's military successes and its unequivocal regional superiority. Later, many of Israel's military failures were attributed to the same undisciplined soldiering and private initiatives that Horowitz had lauded. The break-up of the chain of command occurred during the 1967 War when high-ranking officers, including colonels and major-generals, took over the command of small units and became directly involved in the battles— something Ariel Sharon had done many years before. This mixture of rational military doctrines and practices combined with deeply rooted ideological considerations helped to create a climate in which the war that occurred in 1967, a war which Israel had sought for some time, was an inevitability.

5 Constitution of a *Herrenvolk* Republic

For most Israeli Jews, conquering the entire territory of British colonial Palestine, as well as the Sinai Peninsula (prior to its return to Egypt as the first part of the land for peace deal) and the Syrian (Golan) Heights, was an opportunity to revitalize Israel's character as a frontier and settler-immigrant society. New lands were opened up for Jewish settlement, especially the core territories of the ancient mythological Jewish kingdoms, an essential component of Jewish mythic consciousness. The capture of many Jewish holy places, which had been controlled by the Jordanians prior to 1967, served to strengthen religious and messianic sentiments, chauvinistic orientations, and the settlement-drive within Jewish-Israeli society, factors that would greatly contribute to the coming crisis. The scope, the ease, and the speed of the 1967 victory were perceived even by secular persons as a sign of divine grace and the supremacy of the Jewish presence in the region. Only fear of the demographic consequences of incorporating a large and rapidly growing Arab population within the Jewish state prevented the full *de jure* annexation of the occupied territories. On the one hand, the captured territories were defined as strategically vital for the future defense of Israel, while on the other, they were considered exchangeable for peace.

From the start of the occupation, Fatah and other Palestinian political and guerilla organizations tried to initiate popular resistance and guerilla warfare within the occupied territories, but their efforts met with limited success. Increasing numbers of Palestinian workers began searching for work inside Israel, and within about sixteen years they became the major source of labor in blue-collar trades such as agriculture, construction, and sanitation. Israeli products also inundated the Palestinian consumer market. Even the all-encompassing Arab boycott on Israeli products was bypassed by disguising Israeli products as Arab, and then exporting them to the Arab states by way of the West Bank and Gaza Strip. The economic dependence of the occupied population on Israel—and also the dependence of Israel on the low-skill, low-wage labor market—was established in the post-1967 period and has continued to deepen.

In the post-1967 period, two informal models were simultaneously employed by the Israelis. One was the so-called (Yigal) Allon Plan, which envisioned reshaping Israel's boundaries by establishing frontier settlements on sparsely populated lands in the Jordan Valley. The other model reasoned that Jewish presence must be strengthened in densely populated Palestinian areas in order to avoid any future possibility of giving up part of the Holy Land. This strategy implied that Jewish settlements could not be "uprooted," and that the land on which they were built would become part of the eternal inheritance of the Jewish collectivity. This latter assumption was shown to be completely baseless following the Camp David Peace Accords between Egypt and Israel, in which it was agreed that the exchange of territories for peace is a valid principle.

After the 1977 victory of the rightwing Likud Party, the territories of the Sinai Peninsula were returned to Egypt. At the same time, however, the colonization of the core territories of the biblical Land of Israel—the West Bank—was placed at the top of the national agenda. The major engine behind this colonization effort was the development of a religious and socio-political settler movement called Gush Emunim (Block of the Faithful) and its settlement branch, Ammana.

The rise of Gush Emunim was one ramification of the mass protest movement born from growing discontent in the aftermath of the 1973 War, a war in which Israel was surprised by an attack of Syrian and Egyptian troops that inflicted heavy casualties. The 1973 War brought into question Israeli military superiority in the region and re-emphasized the image of the Israeli state's vulnerability. Between the 1970s and 1990s, the religious hardcore settlers created the territorial infrastructure for a new society in "Judea and Samaria." Territorial settlement was not only part of a national political mission of conquest and occupation, involving the confiscation of "homeland" territories and the expansion of the boundaries of the Israeli state, it also laid the infrastructure for the establishment of a moral community to be run according to the laws of *Halacha* and the judgments of rabbis. It seemed that Gush Emunim stood to conquer not only the mountain area (both geographically and symbolically), but the hearts of the rest of the country's Jewish population. They tried to fashion themselves as a replacement for the secular Sabra kibbutznik fighter-settlers and, more importantly, to take their place as the Zionist avant-garde in Israel. From the areas of Judea and Samaria the message was to spread over the entire country.

The nationalist religious revolutionaries, driven by an aspiration for personal fulfillment, and a burning faith in themselves as representatives of the (perceived) collective interest and the "true and pure Jew," aimed to establish a modern *halachic* state in place of the one that had been corrupted in the previous stages of the "return to Zion." The success of this revolution of faith seemed assured due to the absence of any truly attractive competing ideology that could provide an answer to the political and social situation in the aftermath of the 1967 and 1973 Wars. In this regard, the settlements and the settlers in the occupied territories were just the tip of the iceberg. Religious nationalist individuals and groups who had not settled and were not partners—or were even opposed—to the political activist viewpoint of Gush Emunim became partners in what they viewed as the sublime aspiration of transforming the Israeli state into as Jewish a state as possible. Although Gush Emunim's brand of "Jewishness" was dominated by religious elements, its pioneering spirit, renewed activism, and commitment to the security of the settlements charmed many elite groups, even secular ones. In addition, by opening the frontier and acquiring control over the totality of land that had been the original objective of the Zionistic colonization, Gush Emunim reawakened the dormant codes of the immigrant-settler political culture, which, since 1948, had lost their validity. Thus, the secular elites could become partners with Gush Emunim through a selective empathy with the Jewish religious codex (*Halacha*) and a more central sympathy with Gush Emunim's deeds.

The appearance of the religious nationalistic activism that first challenged the secular socialist political hegemony was preceded by a slow decrease in the power, prestige, and efficiency of state institutions (the military, for example) and, particularly in the aftermath of the 1973 War, a decrease in the centrality of the idea of the state. Gush Emunim's power stemmed from a promise of resurgent state power, which they sanctified and to which they assigned themselves as agents of its interests as they defined them.

As described above, since 1967 Israel has ruled directly—and since 1994 indirectly—over millions of Arab residents lacking all civil and most basic human rights. On the one hand, Israel did not annex the occupied territories and their population (except for East Jerusalem and the Syrian, or Golan, Heights), because it did not want to grant them civil rights—for example, the right to vote and be elected. On the other hand, Israel has freely used all the material and human resources (land, water, etc.) of the territories as if they belonged to the Jewish state. As time passed and this situation became institutionalized, Israel ceased being a true democratic state and became a *Herrenvolk* democracy. This term, coined to describe South Africa under Apartheid, describes a regime in which one group of its subjects (the citizens) enjoys full rights and another group (the non-citizens) enjoys none. The laws of Israel have become the laws of a master people and the morality that of lords of the land. When it is convenient for Israel, residents of the occupied territories are part of the state; when it is not convenient, they are outside the state. The Israeli Government has created a double legal system, a double rule, and a double morality.

It was, however, never unambiguous. Different Israeli political groups deduced different lessons from the 1973 War. One side concluded that peace was a necessity and that Israel must be prepared to make territorial concessions to obtain it (this logic was best represented by the Peace Now movement and other more radical peace activists). As expected, they argued that keeping about 3.5 million Palestinians was dangerous for the ethnic composition and security of the Jewish nation-state. The conclusions and interpretations of the situation from the other side of the political map were that there was no chance for a Jewish polity to be accepted in the region and only its military and political might, including control of as much territory as possible, could ensure its existence. As time passed, the rift between these two attitudes obscured all the other social and political problems of the Israeli state and developed into an overall cultural war. In fact, the internal battle was not only about the geopolitical boundaries of the Jewish state and about the colonization of the occupied territories, but about the entire character of the state and its regime. Moreover, the very existence of the two camps—as well as a relative passivity toward, and even cooperation with, the occupation on the part of a generation of Palestinians—created a long and unique period of *permanent temporaryness* that led to the domestic and international perception that the situation was short-term and reversible. This perception secured time for colonizing at least a part of the territory without any considerable opposition from Israelis, the international community, or the Palestinians themselves.

The political balance of power between the two camps oscillated for a whole generation and depended on various domestic and external events. However, in the long run, as the number and size of the settlements increased, what looked like irreversible facts on the ground enhanced the political power of the chauvinistic and the religious nationalist factions. The increasing political power of the chauvinistic camp also enlarged its capabilities to recruit more human, political, and material resources for their project of expropriating land in the occupied territories. The subject under dispute was not only the number of settlers and settlements, but also their location. The settlers' leaders, with the help of Ariel Sharon, adopted the strategy of spreading the settlements throughout the occupied territories, both to establish a continuum of Jewish territories and to fragment and isolate the Palestinian areas.

Interestingly, the first permanent Jewish presence in the occupied territories—established concomitantly with a settlement at the old station of Sabastia near the Arab city of Hebron, populated by Rabbi Moshe Levinger's weird and ethnocentric group—was a series of Israeli military training bases established by Ariel Sharon in his capacity as the Head of Military Training Schools and later as Minister of Agriculture as well as Minister of National Infrastructures.

By 2002, about 300,000 Jews spread over 160 settlements had colonized the West Bank and Gaza Strip, totaling about 15 percent of the total population of the area. Sixty-five percent of this group lived in several large town-settlements, and most residents were employed inside the Israeli border (or the 1949 ceasefire Green Line). All in all, this colonization drive did not achieve its basic aim of building such a massive Jewish presence in the occupied territories that any possibility of withdrawal would be impossible. This failure seems to stem from the fact that, unlike the early Zionist colonization efforts, this effort did not enjoy broad consensus among the Jewish citizens of Israel. There was, however, enough Jewish settlement activity to threaten to take control of limited Palestinian land and water resources.

There are roughly two types of settlers. About half are ideologically or religiously committed to settle the Land of Israel, and produce a territorial and political *fait accompli*. The other half are Israeli Jews in search of cheaper housing and a higher quality of life (the settlements are heavily subsidized by the government). Although the settlement process was not carried out under the umbrella of a nationwide ideological consensus and was the subject of grave controversy within the Jewish polity, causing a major societal and political cleavage between so-called hawks and doves, no settlements would have been established had the Israeli state not considered these territories an open frontier zone. The former of the two groups believes that Israel must adopt an active and inflexible policy toward the Arabs in general and the Palestinians in particular. This includes the annexation *de facto* or even *de jure* of the lands of Greater Israel, as justified by a mixture of security, nationalist, and/or religious concerns.

6   Childhood in Colonial Palestine

In 1982, Ariel Sharon won worldwide fame and notoriety when, serving as Prime Minister Menachem Begin's Minister of Defense, he became the chief architect of Israel's invasion of Lebanon—the first war between the Israelis and the Palestinians. He was also the Israeli most responsible for the massacres of Palestinian civilians by Israel's Phalangist allies in the Sabra and Shatila refugee camps. Although "Arik"—Ariel Sharon's nickname—became internationally known during the invasion, he had been a cultural hero in Israel, mainly among the youth and the inner circle of the military establishment, since the mid-1950s.

Ariel Scheinerman (Sharon) was born in 1928 in a tiny cooperative village, Kfar Malul, located about fifteen miles northeast of Tel-Aviv in the central area of British colonial Palestine. His childhood was not very happy, mainly because of his father's arrogant and uncooperative behavior toward his neighbors. Many years later, Sharon would write with bitterness in his autobiography that

[the] social tensions [in the village] did not limit themselves to the adults. In a village of so few families, there was no way that the children could avoid feeling them too. I suffered from it, feeling that the friction between my parents and many of their neighbors put a heavy burden on me, that their relationships affected my relationships. I don't know if my friends felt as strongly as I did, but the effects were obvious. The games we played in the fields and orchards stopped at the doors of their houses. I felt isolated and lonely. I wondered what their houses were like inside. The slights hurt deeply and filled me at times with rushes of turbulent emotion.

According to Uzi Benziman, who published a biography of Sharon in 1985, his father armed his six-year-old son with a big bat to defend himself and the family's fields and property. The boy carried it with him for many years, even when he went to school and once, during a childish quarrel, he seriously wounded one his classmates with it. Although his father hired a private tutor for him, the young Sharon was a mediocre student except in fieldcraft and leadership. His classmates did not like him but admired his orienteering skills and leadership ability. During the Second World War, he studied in a Tel Aviv high school. As an adult, he wrote that when he moved to this cosmopolitan city, he was amazed to learn that no one knew about the rifts between his father and the neighbors. He described similar feelings about his first journey to New York City.

His basic attitudes toward the Arabs of Palestine were shaped by the private memories of his parents. It was a mixture of anxiety and scorn. When his mother first arrived in the country, she met "giant" Arab dock workers who took the tender lady from the ship to the coast without any consideration or gentleness. Memoirs written by immigrants during this period often mention the trauma of discovering that the Land of Israel was a country inhabited and ruled by Arabs. One year before Ariel was born, Arab rioters destroyed his small village. This happened again in 1929, and during the Great Arab Revolts of 1936–1939 there were times when the populace were on alert for attacks that never came. These repeated threats became part of the family's collective memory and were deeply etched in young Sharon's mind through family talks.

The basic situation was indeed that most Arabs neither wanted nor welcomed the Jewish settlers and that, since 1918, the local Arabs had developed a relatively efficient anti-Zionist and anti-British national movement. Although many Arabs worked in Jewish colonies and Jewish construction companies or sold land to Jews and Jewish associations, and others maintained good social relationships with Jewish individuals, it was commonly agreed that the Arabs did not accept the notion of Palestine as a "Jewish national home" (a notion brought into existence by the Balfour Declaration) and that the whole collective Jewish existence in the country was based on British bayonets. Added to these tensions were the xenophobic tendencies of both communities, which served to exacerbate the mutual enmity, fear, and hate between Arabs and Jews. This was the atmosphere within which young Ariel Scheinerman was raised, although not everyone growing up in that environment dedicated his life to fighting Arabs, especially after the basic situation changed.

In the 1948 War, Sharon served as an NCO (although he failed to complete a training course given by the Haganah, the Jewish underground militia). He participated in the failed battle of Latrun, a British fortification on the main road from Tel Aviv to Jerusalem. This battle against the Arab Legion is considered, even today, as one of the most serious defeats Israel ever suffered. Hundreds of Israeli soldiers were caught in the crossfire and those who did not escape were slaughtered. Sharon was badly wounded at Latrun and, because of his injuries, was able to participate in only one other battle toward the end of the war.

In this battle, Israeli forces failed to destroy an Egyptian regiment encircled in the so-called Faluja Pocket. After the war, many soldiers and field officers accused the Israeli general staff of gross incompetence and negligence in their management of the conflict, not only because of shameful defeats like Latrun and Faluja, but also because they failed to "liberate" the whole country from Arab domination and left some Arabs within the Jewish state's borders. Sharon was one of those soldiers. While most people soon ceased to accuse the military command and the political leadership of incompetence, of lacking military imagination, of failing to collect adequate intelligence, and even of treason (until the 1973 War that caught Israel unprepared), Ariel Sharon has continued to do so throughout the ups and downs of his long and highly controversial career. These accusations, leveled against superiors, colleagues, and subordinates, have become a permanent part of his rhetoric. For a while he remained in the military, successfully completing a stint as a battalion commander under the guidance of Colonel Yitzhak Rabin and serving as an intelligence officer at the Central and Northern Front Command under Colonel Moshe Dayan. Both these senior officers were deeply impressed by the performance, imagination, and motivation of this young, handsome officer and later intervened several times to save Sharon's military career after he had antagonized superiors with some of his adventurous and irresponsible moves, "imprecise reports," and the ugly personal expressions he used with those who doubted his expertise in any matter connected to the unholy art of war making.

Soon after the 1948 War, disappointed by the military and by what he perceived as an unbearable passivity imposed by the politicians on the armed forces, he left the army and, in 1952, enrolled at the Hebrew University. Even after he became a student, he maintained contact with military buddies and took part as a reserve officer in some minor incidents in the Jerusalem area.

7 Sharon's First Round

In the early 1950s, the Arab–Israeli conflict, exacerbated by the developing Cold War, took on an international dimension once the surrounding Arab states were drawn in. As a condition for recognition of the Jewish state, the Arab states demanded that Israel withdraw to the 1947 Partition Resolution border (which they had previously rejected), and that all Palestinian refugees be returned to their homes. Perceiving these demands as another attempt to annihilate the Jewish state, the Israelis rejected them outright. Israel argued that the Arab countries should absorb the refugees, just as the Jews had absorbed their own refugee brethren. In the meantime, a *petite guerre* developed along the armistice lines. Palestinian infiltrators from the refugee camps in the Gaza Strip and the West Bank harassed the new border settlements, trying to reappropriate property or just to take revenge by killing Israelis. The Israeli government developed a retaliation policy against the host Arab countries, arguing that they should take responsibility for the infiltrations and killings. However, Israel's first reprisals were hampered by the army's poor performance. The military command decided in July 1952 to form a small, highly trained and secret commando unit to handle the reprisal actions. Candidates were recruited discreetly through the old-boy network. Ariel Sharon was appointed commander of the group known as Unit 101.

In his position as commander of Unit 101 (later merged into the Paratroopers Brigade 890 and extended to Paratroopers Division 202), he initiated many military actions that were intended to inflame the Israeli–Jordanian and Israeli–Egyptian lines. With his sharp political instincts, he soon discovered the secret that relatively junior field officers possess more actual power than higher-ranking officers who are far from the battlefield, not to mention civilian politicians who had little knowledge of military affairs yet adored the "new Jewish warriors." A field officer can inflame any border and blow any minor incident out of proportion. All such activities were nominally approved by the command as limited reactions to what Israel perceived as violations of the ceasefire agreements by the Arab states. However, in executing these actions, Sharon went far beyond the scope of what was ordered, planned, and accepted by his superiors. He explained these departures as the result of unexpected resistance by the enemy, unanticipated difficulties and obstacles on the battlefield, and the need to save the lives of Israeli soldiers or to avoid leaving behind the wounded and killed. The fact of the matter was that Sharon's expansive actions caused greater casualties—not only among the Arabs, but among Israeli soldiers as well. His practice of using provocations as a strategy—inciting Arabs and Jews to fight one another—became a major pattern of Sharon's conduct, one that he elaborated on and perfected as his career progressed.

Unit 101's first assignment, in September 1953, was to expel the nomadic Bedouin tribes from the Negev Desert. Traditionally, the Bedouins do not recognize state borders, and even after the 1948 War they moved freely between Jordan, Israel, and Egypt. The Israelis saw these unauthorized border crossings as a violation of their sovereignty over the territory (which was internationally contested during that period anyway). Unit 101's mission was accomplished efficiently and cruelly. Since that first action, Sharon has had two major—from his point of view, successful—clashes with the Bedouins: in the 1970s he expelled many Bedouins from northeastern Sinai in order to make room for Jewish settlers, who Sharon himself later evacuated in 1981 when he was Minister of Defense. Since 2001, he has expelled Bedouins from the South Hebron Mountains, again to prepare the land for Jewish settlements.

Sharon's life-long war against the Arabs in general and the Palestinians in particular started immediately after that first successful operation against the Bedouins. His next major proposal made to command headquarters was a limited raid against the al-Burg refugee camp, which was supposedly used by infiltrators as a base. When he described the details of the operation to his soldiers, one of them—according to Uzi Benziman—observed that the obvious objective of the raid was to kill as many civilians as possible. The soldier complained that this was an improper objective, but Sharon ignored the remark. The result was that fifteen Palestinians were killed, most of them women and children. Interrogated by superiors after the raid, he argued that the high casualty rate was necessitated by the need to defend the lives of his soldiers. He explained to his own soldiers that all the women of the camps were whores that served the murderers. Later the Egyptian authorities, who were made uneasy by the anger and desire for revenge expressed by the Palestinians, channeled these sentiments into the creation of two Palestinian brigades—called Fedayeens—under Egyptian command. The Fedayeens engaged in many guerilla acts inside Israel and later became a prototype and symbolic model for Fatah and other Palestinian guerilla organizations.

Among the dozens of raids executed by the 101 under the command of Ariel Sharon, two are inscribed in both Israeli and Palestinian history and memory. The first was the massacre at Qibiya. Qibiya was a Palestinian village in Jordan (the West Bank) between Latrun and Qalkilliya, which was attacked on October 15, 1953 as a reprisal for the murder of a woman and two children in the Israeli town of Yehud two days before. There had been about 130 Israeli civilian victims of this "border war," and public opinion demanded revenge. About forty-five houses in Qibiya were blown up with their inhabitants inside. Sixty-seven men, women, and children died. Sharon argued during the subsequent investigation that he ordered his soldiers to check every house and warn the inhabitants to leave, but the soldiers denied that they had had such an order.

The operation caused an international uproar and generated questions within important political and intellectual circles. At first, Israel tried to deny that the massacre was carried out by a military unit and claimed that "angry border-area settlers" were responsible. But among the military, the wider population, and especially among the youth, it was considered a big success and raised national pride. Prime Minister

David Ben-Gurion, hearing of the action, suspected that the young commander belonged to a revisionist stream of Zionism, and called him for a talk.[7] During the meeting, Ben-Gurion was very satisfied to discover that Sharon and his family belonged to the "correct" political stream (the Laborite one) and was enchanted by the young, brave, handsome, and bright officer—the embodiment of his vision of the Sabra, a healthy, Israeli-born Jew free from all the maladies of exile. From that time on, the "Old Man," as Ben-Gurion was known, gave Sharon his personal protection and maintained a special relationship with him, which Sharon used every time he got into trouble following one of his adventurous and unauthorized military operations. Moshe Dayan, the recently appointed Commander-in-Chief of the Israeli army, also became an admirer of the brave officer until Sharon ignored his orders and provided him with "imprecise reports," in order to cover-up his disobedience toward superiors. It was also during this period that Ariel Sharon became a hero among the entire Israeli armed forces and the elite high school youths that cultivated a blatant Israeli militarism.

The 1950s were a highly romantic and romanticized period in Israel. In order to understand the role played by Sharon and his Unit 101 (and later by the Paratroopers Brigade and Division), it is essential to understand the spirit of the era. During this period, the Jewish population of the country tripled in size. Newly arrived immigrants, mainly those from Arab lands, endangered the cultural, political

---

7 After the 1948 War, Ben-Gurion purged politically oriented officers from the army, including revisionists and communists with ties to the leftwing Mapam Party, which maintained close ties to the Soviet Union. These purges strengthened his party's (the Mapai) control over the military.

and economic position of the more established Israelis. The military instituted a universal draft for Jews, thereby losing its elite image and ceasing to be a vehicle for mobility and a tool for generating prestige. The "good youth" (the children of the established population), sought ways of preserving their dominance in the rapidly changing country. One of these ways was going to Petra. Petra is an ancient but well-preserved Nabatean city, the ruins of a vanished civilization dotted with the remains of houses and shrines hewn in rocks of changing color, a kind of Middle-Eastern Inca monument. Petra, also known as The Red Rock, is located deep in the Jordanian Desert, and visiting it required many days of walking, mainly at night-time, and carried the risk of being captured or killed by Bedouins or soldiers of the Arab (Jordanian) Legion.[8] As going to Petra became more dangerous and the Bedouins and Legionnaires became more skilled at ambushing and hunting the young Israeli infiltrators, the mission became more attractive. Many Israeli youngsters lost their lives in this adventure but those who succeeded in the journey became unofficial national heroes.

One of these "heroes," Meir Har-Zion, a young man more identified with the Petra myth than others, was also a member of Unit 101. He was considered the ultimate Israeli warrior, a kind of Jewish Rambo. In early 1955, Bedouins assassinated his sister Shoshana, together with her boyfriend Oded Gemeister, during a journey from Jerusalem to Ein-Gedi (a small Israeli settlement south of the Dead Sea), when they took a shortcut onto Jordanian territory. Har-

---

8 A popular singer, Arik Lavie, had a hit called "The Red Rock" that glorified going to Petra and those "who never came back." It was forbidden to broadcast the song for many years to avoid encouraging more young people to risk their lives.

Zion gathered three of his comrades from the 101, caught five suspected Bedouins, and slit their throats. Har-Zion was suspended for six months from military activities as a punishment for his "private operation," but the story spread widely among the young people and just added more glory to Har-Zion, to the 101, and to its commander, Ariel Sharon.

In his autobiography, Sharon wrote that he tried to dissuade Har-Zion from carrying out this act of personal revenge but "I already knew that Meir was not in a state of [mind] to listen to anybody . . . I did what I thought was necessary. I gave him weapons. I gave him a command car and I gave him Yitzhak Ghibli [another colorful hero of the 101] as a driver, the best I had." In sum, Sharon noted, "the entire episode was a throwback to tribal days, the kind of ritual revenge that the Bedouins understood perfectly."

This event exemplifies another trait of the Jewish–Arab conflict, and particularly the Jewish–Palestinian conflict—namely its personification in characters such as Har-Zion. Many outrageous acts were committed by individuals or small groups on both sides who were either engaged in vendettas or thought they knew how to manage the conflict better than the officials. Ariel Sharon was often in this category.

Unit 101, and later the Paratroopers Brigade and Division, were involved in many minor and major retaliatory and pre-emptive operations.[9] The seminal operation, however—one that fundamentally

---

9 Pre-emptive operations were raids initiated by Israel against various targets—military and civilian—on the pretext or hope of reducing or preventing Arab raids into Israel. Israeli strategists argued that the pre-emptive operations prevented major

changed the political realities of the Middle East—was a raid against an Egyptian military base in Gaza in February 1955. During this raid, about forty Egyptian soldiers were killed and many wounded following an ambush planned by Sharon. Eight Israeli paratroopers were also killed. Following this raid, the Egyptian President, Gamal Abd al-Nasser, decided to turn to the Soviet bloc in order to modernize the Egyptian military with new weapons (mainly the well-known fighter jet the Mig-21 and T-type tanks) and military advisors. Thus was born the Czech–Egyptian military treaty that led to an intensive regional arms race, complemented by a similar Franco–Israeli pact that lasted until France was involved in Algeria in its cruel war against the Front de Libération National. For Nasser, making a deal with the Communist Bloc was neither easy nor without disadvantages. During the period when the Cold War was escalating, he made considerable efforts to constitute with Pandit Nehru and Tito a neutral Third Bloc. He had hoped to make Egypt, under his leadership, the leader of the Arab world (his second circle in his "Three Circles doctrine"—Egypt, the Arab world, and the unaligned countries) but the treaty with Czechoslovakia undermined this ambition, reducing Egypt to the status of a client and satellite of the Soviet Union.

But the raid on Gaza was just the beginning. In December 1955, Sharon's paratroopers attacked Syrian forces situated on the eastern shore of the Sea of Galilee (the Kinneret). Close to sixty Syrian soldiers were killed and thirty taken prisoner. During an additional

---

regional wars. In fact, they only escalated the conflict and caused two wars, in 1956 and 1967.

raid on the Egyptian base at Quintile, ten Egyptians were killed and twenty taken prisoner.

The mid-1950s were probably the happiest and most glorious days in Sharon's military career. Most of his plans for military actions (and Sharon is well known as a prolific, compulsive, and highly imaginative tactician and planner) were accepted by the military command and the government, although maybe not to the extent to which he later implemented them. His actions were met with mixed feelings by both his military superiors and by civilian officials, but nobody had the guts to argue with success.

There is no doubt that his unrestrained retaliations and preventive-strike policy helped to worsen the Arab–Israeli crisis and to bring about two wars. Uzi Benziman depicted Sharon as solely responsible for a premeditated escalation of the conflict, designed to provoke a regional war (probably in order to complete the "unfinished job" of 1948).

8   An Officer but Not a Gentleman

The aim of the present essay is not to provide another biography of Ariel Sharon, but to describe and analyze his relations with the Palestinian people within their wider context and kaleidoscopic cultural background. Sharon's ascension to power is also regarded as the climax of a generation-long internal crisis within Israeli society. As such, a short review of Sharon's life between 1956 and 1982 will lead to a better understanding of events within Israeli society. The myths and the legends created by Sharon himself, by journalists like his life-long servant Uri Dan, and by other admirers and public-relations experts, depict this period as a uniquely successful and glorious era in the life of a military mastermind. In fact, it was a time of serial military and human-relations failures.

A case in point was Sharon's performance while serving as the commander of a paratrooper brigade deployed during the Suez War. On October 29, 1956, Israel, in cooperation with France and Britain, invaded the Sinai Peninsula.[10] Sharon's paratroopers were sent to the Mitla Pass, 140 miles behind Egyptian lines, to fulfill two objectives: first, to prevent the Egyptians from sending reinforcements toward the advancing Israeli infantry, and second, to disguise the main objectives and scope of the military operation. Sharon refused to carry out the orders given to him by command headquarters, tried on his own to break through the Pass toward the Suez Canal, and led his forces into an Egyptian trap. All three

10 Gamal Abd al-Nasser had infuriated British and French decision makers by nationalizing the Suez Canal. The French also suspected that Egypt helped the Arab Algerian rebels both militarily and financially. The initial plan was that the Israeli invasion would provide the two countries with a pretext to intervene and demand both Egyptian and Israeli withdrawal from the canal zone. The British and French military were supposed to take over the canal area but the ultimate aim was to overthrow Nasser and his regime. Israel conquered the Sinai Peninsula rapidly, mainly because the Egyptians' priority was the defense of the canal and the Egyptian interior, which they handled well. The British and French armies were rapidly defeated and forced to withdraw under the combined pressure of the United States and the Soviet Union. This was the only time during the Cold War that the superpowers cooperated to restore the world's established hierarchy. Israel's apparent victory was reduced to getting some UN forces located between it and Egypt and regaining free navigation in the Red Sea (Sharm a-Sheik Pass and Tiran Strait), which had been closed by Egypt in 1955—an action considered by Israel to be a *casus belli*. Because of the war, however, Israel did gain a self-image and an international reputation as a regional military power.

components of any military operation—command, communication, and control (the three Cs)—collapsed. Encircled by Egyptians hiding in the surrounding mountains, the paratrooper unit fought a cruel, day-long battle to escape from the ambush. Twenty-eight soldiers were killed and more than a hundred were wounded in this unnecessary battle. After the War, fellow officers accused Sharon of initiating this operation solely to gain personal fame. Sharon engaged in these types of actions in war after war, causing great controversy among the military commanders. Describing these controversies in his autobiography, he attributed them to his colleagues' envy and lack of military skills and imagination. After the Mitla affair, his military career was stalled for years, and when he was finally promoted to the rank of colonel he was assigned to fill marginal, non-combatant roles, in spite of Ben-Gurion's strenuous efforts to help him. Sharon described his four years away from active command as years of frustration and exile.

However, before his exile, Dayan compensated him by sending him to study at a military college in Surrey, England. Sharon described the time he spent there as a decisive influence in the formulation of his military thinking. Comparing the tactics used by the British and German commands in the Western Desert during World War II, he found that the German military model used by Rommel was far superior to the British model used by Montgomery. The famous British military expert Basil Liddell Hart concurred with this analysis and, since that time, Sharon has considered himself to be Israel's greatest military thinker.

Only seven years later in 1964, when Yitzhak Rabin was Chief of Staff, Sharon was promoted to a position at the command headquarters of the Northern Front, where he tried to initiate an aggressive military policy against Syria. Because his fellow commanders, including the general staff, did not see any reason to inflame the border and risk a full-scale war with Syria, most of his plans were rejected, although he did regain his fame as a brave and original officer. Rabin promoted him to the rank of major-general but sent him back to a non-combatant position. At the same time, he was also given command of a reserve division. From this position, he served as an extremely successful military commander in the 1967 War.

In May 1967, Gamal Abd al-Nasser made his biggest political miscalculation. After a long and bloody intervention in the Yemeni civil war, he had lost prestige in the Arab world. In order to regain that prestige and affirm Egyptian sovereignty, he made two spectacular moves: he ordered Egyptian military forces to cross the Suez Canal and, at the same time, demanded the withdrawal of UN forces deployed along the 1957 ceasefire lines. After the Yemeni debacle, the Egyptian army was certainly not ready for a war with Israel, but the Israeli General Staff had planned for many years to destroy the Egyptian military, which had been re-equipped and restructured by the Soviet Union after the 1956 War. Nasser's move was exploited by the Israeli Government, which depicted it as a *casus belli* and a real threat to Israel's security. The Israeli armed forces mobilized their full reserve system. While the two armies were positioned face-to-face, the Israeli Government, headed by Levy Eshkol, hesitated, doubting both the reality of the Egyptian threat and the necessity of resolving it militarily rather than diplomatically. Another consideration was the severe economic hardship and social strain that would result from the prolonged mobilization of almost the entire male labor force. While the government weighed its options, military officers (including Sharon) seized the opportunity to convince the public that Israel faced a genuine threat to its existence. Demonstrations called on Eshkol to quit. The increasing public pressure in addition to the hidden pressure from many on the general staff led to the establishment of a new war-oriented Cabinet that included the hawkish Moshe Dayan as Minister of Defense and, for the first time, members of the ultra-nationalist party Herut, headed by Menachem Begin.[11] The war was so well planned and prepared that at dawn, on June 5, the Israeli military intelligence and air force knew the precise location of every Egyptian, Syrian, and Jordanian aircraft and destroyed most of them on the ground in several hours. Sharon, in his autobiography, briefly mentioned that "on the morning of June 5, Israel's air force was to launch a pre-preemptive attack on Egypt's airfields." When Israeli infantry and tank brigades attacked Egyptian military concentrations, fortifications, and bases, they already had almost absolute air superiority. One of the most significant myths rooted in the collective memory of both the Israeli and Western

11 Both Yitzhak Rabin and Ezer Weizman clearly allude in their autobiographies to the fact that, prior to the attack of June 1967, the Israeli general staff organized a putsch, and barred any and all political solutions to the crisis. Rabin, Chief of Staff, admitted that: "Nasser didn't want war. The two divisions he sent to Sinai would not have been sufficient to launch an offensive war. He knew it and we knew it" (*Le Monde*, February 28, 1968). Levy Eshkol himself admitted that "the Egyptian layout in Sinai and the general build up there testified to a militarily defensive Egyptian set-up, south of Israel" (*Yediot Ahronot*, October 16, 1967). On August 8, 1982, Prime Minister Menachem Begin, defending the invasion of Lebanon, said: "In June 1967 we again had a choice. The Egyptian army concentrations in the Sinai did not prove that Nasser was really about to attack us. We must be honest with ourselves. We decided to attack him" (*New York Times*, August 21, 1982).

public is that during the 1967 War (or as the Israelis arrogantly called it, "the Six Day War"), Egypt and Syria attacked Israel, a belief that is used to justify the legitimacy of the occupation to this day.[12]

Sharon commanded one of the three divisions that led a surprise assault on Egyptian forces in the Sinai. His objective was the important Egyptian military compound at Abu-Agella, situated on the main road through the Sinai. This decisive battle, which destroyed a major portion of Egypt's military forces, was unprecedented in an important respect: its kill ratio. Thousands of Egyptians were killed while Israeli forces sustained few casualties. Probably, Sharon reasoned that military equipment could be easily replaced (by the Soviets) but that training efficient military units could take years. Later, in another battle deeper in the Sinai, Sharon surrounded an Egyptian tank battalion at Nakl and destroyed it completely. Here again, about a thousand Egyptian solders were killed. No doubt, from a strictly military point of view, Sharon proved his ability to plan and conduct complex military operations during the 1967 War, and his public image as Israel's number-one warrior was assured. However, Sharon's aims went beyond being a military hero. He obviously observed how men like Yigal Allon and Moshe Dayan (both considered candidates

12 On the first day of the war, and following Egyptian announcements of imaginary victories, the Jordanians hesitantly attacked some localized points in Israel, both because they wanted to demonstrate solidarity with Egypt and because they wanted to share in the post-war plunder. The main attack was in Jerusalem, a traditionally disputed area between the Hasemits and the Israelis since 1948. Israel warned Jordan not to join the war, but the warning was ignored. In 1973, Jordan warned Israel about the coordinated attack prepared by Egypt and Syria, but for various reasons, the Israeli government ignored the warning. After defeating the Egyptian army, Israel used the opportunity to conquer the West Bank (of the Jordan).

for the premiership) converted their military past into political assets. His headquarters was always filled by groupies—journalists, mediocre writers, and PR people who mythologized him in exchange for being known as his emissaries.

Sharon's first assignment after the war was as General Commander of Military Training Schools and Bases. In this capacity, and contrary to the will of his superiors, he ordered the transfer of the entire system of military training bases to the recently occupied West Bank. By establishing a huge military presence on these territories, Sharon built the necessary infrastructure (roads, electricity, and thousands of Israeli soldiers) for the colonization of the occupied territories.

During these first post-war years, Egypt and Israel fought the so-called War of Attrition along the Suez Canal. Following the Chief of Staff Haim Bar-Lev's idea, Israel built a fortification line to control the area. Egypt bombarded this line with heavy artillery for three years while Israel responded with artillery, bomber aircraft, and occasional raids on the west bank of the canal. Both sides suffered heavy casualties during this period. Sharon and a handful of other officers like Israel Tal and Matitiyahu Peled suggested, no doubt correctly from a professional point of view, an alternative means of holding the line: a flexible and mobile force located about fifteen miles from the canal but able to rapidly counter-attack any Egyptian force that crossed the canal, without themselves being within the effective range of Egyptian artillery. The issue of how to hold the canal became a major controversy within the general command but was also the object of a personal quarrel between Sharon and most of his colleagues in the "pit" (the nickname for the Israeli underground headquarters of the general command). Sharon constantly accused his superiors and colleagues in the pit of ignorance, stupidity, and responsibility for Israel's heavy casualties (close to 1,500 by August 1970, with about 360 deaths among them). Sharon, as usual, leaked the controversy to the press using his admirers in the media to defame his colleagues. When Sharon forgot to fill out some forms, Bar-Lev decided to use this bureaucratic mistake as a pretext for getting rid of him. Dayan and Golda Meir avoided intervening, and Sharon turned to the opposition leaders with a proposal to join them in the coming election. Sharon was the first, and probably will not be the last, Israeli general to conduct party talks while still in uniform—which was a major violation of the rules but a brilliant political move. When the strong man of the ruling party (Finance Minister Pinchas Sapir) was informed that a popular general might join the opposition, he took the necessary measures to keep Sharon in the army. Moreover, he was appointed to one of the most important positions in the military hierarchy—the Commander of the Southern Front.

Between 1967 and 1970, the Palestinians in the Gaza Strip's refugee camps engaged in sporadic armed resistance against the Israeli occupation. In August 1970, Sharon began mopping up remnant guerilla cells. He operated systematically and with great brutality, moving from neighborhood to neighborhood and from grove to grove. The army imposed day-long curfews and gathered the entire population of a neighborhood or refugee camp (preferred sites were the Shatti and Jebalia camps), thus enabling the soldiers to make house-to-house searches and ensuring easy access for the military to any part at the Gaza Strip. This meant demolishing thousands of homes and uprooting large portions of the Gaza Strip's citrus groves, the region's only crop. Orders were given to shoot any suspect without trial or inquiry, and over a thousand people were duly shot dead or executed. These collective punishments of civilian populations and extra-judicial executions were strictly forbidden by international laws, which defined them as war crimes. Although this system, which has recently been applied to other parts of the occupied territories, created unease among Sharon's own officers and soldiers as well as the general staff, it was backed by Minister of Defense Moshe Dayan. This was Sharon's first major involvement with the Palestinian problem. Seven months later, he was relieved of his responsibility for the Gaza Strip.

From the very first months of the occupation, Israel proudly declared that it would administer the "most enlightened occupation" (a contradiction in terms, by the way) by giving inhabitants of the occupied territories full local autonomy without any Israeli intervention. In other words, they could provide their own basic municipal services such as education and electricity. In fact, during the immediate post-war period, the Israeli Cabinet was certain that the superpowers would not allow them to hold most of the territory and would impose a withdrawal, just as they had in 1957.

Under this presumption, one week after the end of the war, on June 19, 1967, the Israeli National Unity Government, which included Menachem Begin, decided unanimously to suggest returning all captured Egyptian and Syrian territories in exchange for a full peace. The decision was passed to the United States, which was expected to act as a go-between. However, according to new evidence provided by Israeli researcher Dan Babli, the US never delivered the message, presumably because they were not interested in reopening the Suez Canal or in providing other benefits to Soviet client states.

In the summer of 1968, the leaders of the Arab states, who had never received the Israeli message, held a conference in Khartoum. The conference was concluded with the notorious "three no's" to Israel: no negotiation, no recognition, and no peace. The statement reflected the traditional Arab attitude of not recognizing a Jewish state's right to exist in the region. The Israelis read the Khartoum summit declaration as a response to their peace message and buried their own initiative as if it had never been made.

In 1968, the political situation in Israel remained fluid and unclear. On the one hand, the population and leadership were still euphoric after the "miraculous" victory which was presented as the result of an imposed and unavoidable pre-emptive war that saved Israel from total annihilation. On the other hand, in contrast with the well-planned war, the Israeli leadership and political elite had no idea what to do with the occupied territories and especially not with the people who suddenly fell under Israeli control. Prime Minister Levy Eshkol tried to negotiate with Palestinian notables from the West Bank and Gaza about the possibility of granting them autonomy with or without their sharing authority with the Jordanian regime. However, the local Palestinian leadership made it clear that they did not feel authorized to negotiate with the Israelis and proclaimed that the sole legitimate representative of the Palestinian people was the Palestine Liberation Organization, an unthinkable idea at that time for the Israelis.

Although the Israeli Government was unsure of what to do with the occupied territories, Ariel Sharon began establishing facts on the ground. He and Dayan shared the idea that the Gaza Strip should be separated forever from Egyptian (and Palestinian) control. They agreed that thousands of Bedouins should be uprooted from northern

Sinai and Rafah and that those areas should be prepared for Jewish settlement. Vast territories were fenced and water wells were clogged. Thus, Dayan and Sharon tried to decide alone, without consulting the Cabinet or the Knesset, on the future of these areas and perhaps the future of the entire region. Dayan even pushed a personal project to build a new city on the edge of the Sinai—Yamit. This project was enlarged to make room for Jewish settlements within the Gaza Strip itself. Benziman writes that the cooperation between Dayan and Sharon was so perfect that the Minister of Defense never had to give any written orders to the general, he had only to express wishful thinking about an issue (for example, "How nice it would be if there were no Bedouins in a certain area"), and Sharon would consider it an order.[13] For the first and last time during his military career, Sharon became an obedient soldier. The actions implemented by Sharon were retroactively justified by "security considerations," an ever-popular argument within all parts of the Israeli political culture, even the judicial branch. When displaced Bedouins sought redress from the Israeli High Court of Justice, their petition was rejected after Sharon appeared in court personally with "data" citing "security concerns."

The close collaboration between Sharon and Dayan led Sharon to believe that a position as Commander-in-Chief was all but guaranteed to him. However, both the newly appointed Chief of Staff David

---

13 Conventional histories based almost solely on written or recorded documents normally ignore the fact that powerful and sophisticated decision makers are usually quite careful about which documents remain behind and how these documents will depict them in the light of history. From this point of view, many historians are no more than servants of past and present powers.

Elazar and Prime Minister Golda Meir insisted that Sharon terminate his active military duties, in part because Meir saw him as a danger to Israeli democracy. Sharon promptly resigned and on July 15, 1973 was released from active military service, though not from reserve duties.

Sharon began his political career immediately with a wide media campaign emphasizing two major motifs: that he was forced to resign from the military against his will for political reasons, and that in spite of Israel being a regional military power, its "cowardly" government avoided using military force to achieve (unspecified) political goals. At the same time, he joined the Liberal Party, a partner in Mahal, one of the Knesset's rightwing blocs that also included Begin's Herut Party. Sharon invested a lot of energy in uniting these parties and adding additional smaller factions in order to create a new party running under the slogan "unity in the defense of Greater Israel." Sharon believed that if he united all these opposition parties before the election, the new coalition could replace the "eternal" ruling party and appoint him as Minister of Defense. However, Sharon's attempts were abortive, either because he was still an inexperienced political outsider or because the politicians involved distrusted each other.

While Sharon was attempting to cobble a political movement together, the 1973 War erupted. Tens of thousands of Egyptian infantry soldiers and hundreds of tanks crossed the Suez Canal and the Bar-Lev Line collapsed. In the north, the Syrian military, which had coordinated its attack with Egypt, seized the Golan Heights and threatened to invade northern Israel. Contrary to conventional wisdom, the attack was not a surprise. The Israeli military and other intelligence sources had received precise warnings that had mentioned both the day and the hour. King Hussein himself informed Golda Meir about the coming attack. The presumption was that if Israel were to let Egypt and Syria know that it was fully informed about the attack plans, the war could be postponed or even averted.

Israel's failure to prevent the expected war can be explained as the result of an informal meeting in the legendary "Golda's kitchen," an account of which was recently published by Hanoch Bartov.[14] The meeting, which took place about six months before the start of the war, included Golda Meir, Moshe Dayan, and Israel Gallili, a minister without portfolio and Meir's chief advisor and mastermind. Gallili reported at the meeting that if Israel did not respond to what he described as "generous proposals" made by Sadat, war was unavoidable. Both Meir and Dayan responded with a "so what?" explaining that an attack would give Israel a chance to destroy the Soviet-equipped army for the second time. Thus, arrogantly, Israel expected a war, but not the one that actually developed. The surprise was on the tactical level. Thousands of Egyptian solders held light wire-guided Sagger missiles that badly damaged the Israeli air force and armored units, almost completely paralyzing them during the first phase of the war. The west bank of the canal was also defended with dense long-range surface-to-air missile batteries that were destroyed only later by the armored and infantry forces that crossed the canal westward.

14 It had been common knowledge for a long time that Israel knew in advance about the 1973 War and did nothing to prevent it; however, Bartov, in his new, enlarged edition of David (nicknamed "Dado") Elazar's biography, provided hard documentary evidence.

Ariel Sharon and his reserve division (143) were mobilized without delay as the Egyptians and Syrians easily broke Israeli lines and besieged Israeli strongholds along the canal. But in this war Sharon explicitly fought on two fronts: one against the Egyptian forces in the south and the other for his own personal glory, which he hoped to convert into political gains after the war. Sharon's aim was to be the first to cross the Suez Canal from the east and to be recognized by the Israeli public as the main, if not the only, hero who won the war and saved Israel from catastrophe. He wanted to achieve this aim by any means necessary and regardless of any other considerations. During this war, Sharon was accused by his colleagues of ignoring most of the orders given by the supreme commanders and the general staff and of disrupting any plan not in accordance with his personal interest. He left the flanks of his own and other Israeli units uncovered in order to be the first to cross the canal. He was also determined to beat his rival, fellow division commander General Abraham Adan, who was originally assigned by command headquarters to cross the Suez Canal at the proper time as part of a planned counter-offensive.[15] Sharon's division was supposed to open a road to the canal, establish and protect a bridgehead on the west bank, and shield General Adan's forces during their crossing of the canal.

On October 9, a small reconnaissance unit from Sharon's division discovered an undefended space between the Second and Third

15 The 1973 War was labeled "the war of generals" among the generals themselves, who were deeply concerned about how the evaluations of their successes and failures would reflect on their professional prestige. While other senior officers were mainly concerned about their place in history, Sharon had an immediate political agenda.

Egyptian Armies, which were crossing the canal eastward. Sharon, whose units were still not fully manned or equipped, asked the general staff's permission to exploit the space between the two Egyptian armies and cross the canal, causing confusion among the Egyptian armed forces and command. Sharon's suggestion, which was regarded as extremely hazardous, was rejected for two reasons. First, the small forces Sharon had at his disposal, which were supported by only a few tanks and lacked proper air cover, could be easily destroyed by the huge concentrations of Egyptian forces in the area. Second, the military leadership expected a general Egyptian offensive against Israel—which did in fact happen—and decided not to disperse Israeli forces which were still undermanned and not fully equipped. For the same reason, the command rejected Sharon's earlier suggestion that his division lead an expedition to rescue the desperate besieged soldiers on the canal line. In mid-October, it was finally possible for Sharon to cross the canal. His ambition to cross the canal first led to many unnecessary Israeli casualties, caused several brigades to become vulnerable to attack, and led to many soldiers rushing deep into Egyptian territory without sufficient support, ammunition, and equipment. Sharon suffered a minor wound to his forehead and a photograph of the bleeding Israeli General riding on African soil and circled by admiring soldiers chanting "Arik, King of Israel" was spread across the country and around the world. In spite of Sharon's highly controversial military decisions, he became known once again as the "savior of Israel."

9 The Patron of the Settlers

Promptly after the ceasefire agreements with Egypt and Syria, Israel
was swamped by waves of protests, originating for the first time in
the middle class. Returning soldiers told the people not only about
the horrors of war, but about the military command's poor prepara-
tions, confusion, and lack of leadership. Protesters demanded
responsibility and accountability from the political echelons too,
namely Golda Meir and Moshe Dayan. Popular protests grew even
though the people were far from knowing the complete truth about
how much the civilian leadership was responsible for this costly and
bloody war. New terms were introduced into the political discourse
and public agenda like *mehdal*, the failure to anticipate and prepare
for the war that was so obviously coming, and *kontzeptia*, the
misconception that, under the currently existing territorial and geopolitical circumstances, the Arabs would never have the incentive to
attack Israel. These terms reflected how little the public and even the
elite knew about the real cause of the war, which claimed the lives of
2,636 Israelis and thousands of Egyptian and Syrian soldiers. It must
be noted that until the meaning and consequences of the 1973 War
were fully digested, the vast majority of Israeli Jewish citizens were
unconcerned by the problems inherent in holding 3.5 million Palestinian Arabs in the occupied territories, perhaps because the situation
was still considered to be temporary.

From the sociological point of view the military occupation of a
territory is a unique social order, a regime temporarily managed by a
foreign power following a war. Under such a regime, most or all of

the population's civil and political rights are suspended but, since the nineteenth century, their human rights are supposedly protected by international conventions and laws. Occupations are supposed to be temporary because it is assumed to be unbearable to deny a population its civil rights or, alternatively, its right of self-determination. An occupation can be ended in three ways: by the withdrawal of the occupying forces and the restoration of the original social order; by granting self-determination to the population of the territory; or by the annexation of the territory to the occupier and granting, at least formally, the same rights to the appropriated population that citizens of the occupying power enjoy. International law recognizes the right to resist occupation, but under strict rules, forbidding, for example, the intentional killing of civilians.

In Israel the discourse about the future of the occupied territories was conducted among a handful of elite groups and between politicians. After 1973, the public not only abandoned its post-1967 euphoria but also became increasingly aware of the complexity of their situation. The great amorphous popular protest movement split slowly in two opposite directions and formed two extra-parliamentary, highly articulated movements. One group decided that, owing to a mixture of nationalistic, religious, and security reasons, all conquered land, or at least the whole territory of historical Palestine plus the Syrian Golan Heights, should be annexed permanently by Israel. This group also believed that the territories had to be settled (colonized is a more accurate term under these circumstances) by a grass-roots movement in order to force the state not to give them up.

In order to pacify the citizens after the disastrous 1973 War, the

Cabinet established a committee of inquiry headed by the respected High Court Judge Shimon Agranat. The committee's aims were defined narrowly and related only to the actions of military commanders during a certain period. The commission found only the Chief of Staff David Elazar, the Commander of the Southern Front Shmuel Gonen, and the Chief of Military Intelligence to be responsible for the mishandling of the war and they were dismissed.

In a belated election held in December 1973, the public was still unprepared to punish the ruling party for its negligence and failure, in spite of the large popular protest. This protest was partially provoked by Sharon's vociferous accusations against the military and political leadership and its policies, and in particular by the interim agreement with Egypt for the redeployment of military forces—an agreement that later formed the basis for the peace accords. During the war, Sharon had opposed accepting the United Nations ceasefire resolution. Concerned about eroding Israeli deterrence capabilities, he had demanded that the fighting continue until Israel had achieved a decisive victory over Egypt. During this election, the rightwing opposition party Likud, although still fragmented, considerably increased its power in the Knesset, going from 29 to 39 seats out of 120. One of the Likud seats was held by Ariel Sharon.

Sharon found that the gray parliamentary work of an opposition party backbencher did not suit his temperament, character, and ambitions. He was also hampered by the mutual suspicion and distrust that developed between veteran politicians and the highly opinionated newcomer. He resigned when a resolution was passed forbidding any Knesset member from holding a high-ranking position as a field commander. In fact, Sharon had searched continuously for an opportunity to return to active military service and to be promoted to the position he desired most, Chief of Staff of the Israeli armed forces. Golda Meir's resignation, the nomination of Yitzhak Rabin as premier, the intensification of the Israeli–Palestinian struggle along the Israeli border, and the purge of the general staff following the Agrant Committee's findings were all perceived by Sharon as an opportunity to seek a more active role in defining Israel's military policy.

After the expulsion of Fatah and the other Palestinian guerilla organizations from Jordan following bloody clashes in September 1970, the PLO took control of territory in southern Lebanon, gradually establishing a state within a state. Their headquarters were located in the Fakahani neighborhood of West Beirut. From their bases in southern Lebanon, Palestinian guerilla organizations launched a series of raids against mainly civilian targets both inside and outside of Israel.

These raids began in the mid-1960s and continued for two decades. Numbering in their hundreds, the raids caused heavy casualties, many among civilians. However, most cases of multi-casualty terrors were consequences of failed rescue operations by Israeli military and police units, who tried to free hostages being used as bargaining chips to secure freedom for Palestinian fighters held in Israeli jails or camps. The Israeli security forces' action at Avivim (May 20, 1970), in which nine children were killed and nineteen injured, and Ma'alot (May 15, 1974), in which twenty-one children were murdered and sixty-eight injured, were both examples of tragedies where casualties were caused, in part, by failed rescue efforts. A third example occurred on March 11, 1978, when an attempt to rescue passengers aboard a hijacked bus led to thirty-five people being killed, most of whom were from small, poor frontier settlements.

The attacks by various Palestinian groups were not confined to Israeli territory but were directed at Israeli targets around the world. Members of the Israeli Olympic team were taken hostage in Munich on November 5, 1972. During the abortive rescue operation led by German security units, eleven Israeli athletes were killed. On many occasions Palestinian guerilla organizations cooperated with other organizations, like the German Baader-Meinhof Gang, the IRA, and the Japanese Red Army. Thus, a Japanese Red Army unit in cooperation with the Popular Front for the Liberation of Palestine hit Ben-Gurion International Airport in an action named Operation Deir Yassin, killing sixteen people and injuring seventy-six. Even more frightening were the worldwide attacks on airliners during which Palestinian guerillas would hijack planes and sometimes explode them in mid-air. This intolerable assault against the entire international community was executed mainly, although not exclusively, by smaller Palestinian guerilla organizations.

Terror is most often the weapon of the weak against strong organizations like states, which may be regional or world powers. However, as is demonstrated in this present volume, it also includes the use of indiscriminate violence against civilians in order to achieve military and political goals. Moreover, the label "terror" is subject to interpretation. What one side in a conflict would call terror might be regarded by the other side as legitimate resistance to occupation, as well as ethnic, religious, or national oppression. The very battle to define the situation (e.g., "terrorism" versus "resistance" or "armed struggle") is a part of the conflict, in this case between the Israelis and

Palestinians. However, it must be stated unequivocally that the intentional killing of unarmed civilians, or the deliberate exposure of them to situations in which they can be killed, is a war crime and a crime against humanity. It is morally wrong, whether it is used by non-state and underground organizations or by a "legitimate" state apparatus. The same principle applies to the extra-judicial killings of terror suspects by states (see the second part of this volume), including Israel, the United States, and Britain.

It may seem that by adopting this moral position, we risk placing ourselves in a moral bind. When there is an immense asymmetry of power between weak and stateless ethnic groups (like the Palestinians) and strong powers (like Israel), defining legitimate resistance in limited ways seems to benefit the powerful party in the dispute and the status quo. But as we shall see later, this problem is only apparent and not real.

On the one hand, terrorist attacks made the Israeli–Palestinian problem an important part of international politics and contributed to the reformulation of the Palestinian issue from a humanitarian refugee problem into a re-politicized national claim for self-determination. On the other hand, the terrorist attacks created Israel's existential need, or pretext, to commit politicide against the Palestinian people, expressed and represented at present most vividly by Ariel Sharon. By engaging in terrorist attacks, the frustrated and desperate Palestinians tried to draw international attention to their cause and to force the Israelis to negotiate with them, but their armed struggle provoked severe retaliation from the Israelis, created a suspicion that they were not ready to reach peaceful agreement, and was strongly condemned by most of the international community. These tactics stigmatized the Palestinians as bloodthirsty terrorists and subhumans, with whom any *rapprochement* or understanding was out of the question, and let Israel justify its continuous and increasing oppression of them as self-defense. More recently, terrorist attacks have created a domestic political climate in Israel that makes a second Nakba more likely.[16]

In 1976 Sharon crossed political lines again, left the Likud, and joined the government of Labor Prime Minister Rabin as a special advisor for eight months, beginning in June. In his autobiography, Sharon summed up this period:

> It had been a fruitful time, giving me experience at a level which was new for me, forcing me to consider national issues from the perspective of a sitting prime minister, putting me in contact with world leaders. It was with Rabin that I first met Henry Kissinger, who looked at me and growled jovially, "I hear you are the most dangerous man in the Middle East."

Despite Sharon's idyllic description of this period, Rabin did not give him carte blanche for his own initiatives and even excluded him from access to a lot of information; still, this was indeed an important

16 In July 1974, the Twelfth Palestinian National Council adopted the idea of establishing "a Palestinian national authority in any area liberated from Israeli control," the so-called mini-state option. Faced with this resolution and the possibility of Palestinian participation in the Geneva Peace Conference, Israel claimed that this far-reaching PNC resolution was another plot to destroy Israel. Incidentally, this resolution prompted George Habash, the leader of The Popular Front for the Liberation of Palestine, to resign from the PLO Executive Committee and establish, along with Syrian guerilla groups, the Rejectionist Front.

period for him. He developed a master plan for Jewish settlement in the occupied territories, aiming to create facts on the ground that would make it impossible to remove Jewish control over the territories. During his service as Rabin's advisor, Sharon devoted time to developing a strategic view of the Palestinians. Perhaps for the first time, Sharon regarded the Palestinians not solely through the gun sight but from a wider geopolitical perspective. He elaborated the basic idea of letting the Palestinians establish their own state in Jordan but eliminating their political, military, and social presence in Lebanon. To further these aims, he established his first links with Major Sa'ad Haddad, the commander of a pro-Israeli militia in southern Lebanon. Sharon even broke an important Israeli taboo by repeatedly declaring his willingness to collaborate with the PLO in making Jordan the new Palestinian state. He identified the Christian Maronites of Lebanon as "natural allies" of Israel (after civil strife erupted in Lebanon) against the Palestinians. After the 1977 electoral upheaval that led to his appointments as Minister of Agriculture and Chairman of the Settlement Committee, and later as Minister of Defense, he tried to implement these ideas.

One of Sharon's policies implemented during his term as Minister of Defense failed miserably: the establishment of an anti-PLO armed militia called the Village League under the direction of an Israeli civilian administrator and Hebrew University professor, Menachem Milson. Ironically, during this same period, Israelis administering the occupied territories and acting on the advice of orientalist experts supported traditional Islamic elements because they were considered more easily managed and submissive to the Israelis than the PLO nationalists.

Rabin's government fell within a short time because of both a minor

incident with the National Religious Party and because Rabin possessed
an unauthorized bank account in New York. A new election was
fixed for May 17, 1977, and Sharon, unable to return to Likud, ran
with his own party, Shlomzion, and won two seats. But the major
outcome of this election was the massive defeat of the Labor Party,
mainly because it lost votes to a newly formed, middle-class, centrist
party, Dash (an acronym for Democratic Movement for Change),
which was headed by respectable archeology professor and TV star
Yigael Yadin, the officer who had formulated and executed Plan D. In
accordance with Israeli law, the head of the party drawing the largest
number of votes, this time Menachem Begin, became prime minister
after successfully assembling a coalition. Ariel Sharon's tiny party
merged with Likud, and he was given the portfolio of Minister of
Agriculture. Moshe Dayan, who had crossed party lines, was rewarded
with an appointment as Minister of Foreign Affairs, and Ezer Weizman
(the commander of the air force during the 1967 War) became Minister
of Defense.

In this Cabinet Sharon became one of the settlers' major patrons,
serving with greater élan than Shimon Peres, whom he replaced. In
his autobiography, he boasted that during his first four years as
minister, *he* managed to establish sixty-four settlements in the occupied territories.

At this point, it is necessary to emphasize that according to clause
fifty-five of the 1907 Hague Convention, occupying powers will act
only as temporary managers and beneficiaries of land and other
properties in occupied territories; the creation of permanent facts on
the ground is not permitted. An example of such a fact is the
transference of a population from the occupying country to occupied

territories. Thus, all the Jewish settlements in the territories are illegal according to international law and are at best temporary.[17]

In the summer of 1980, both Moshe Dayan and Ezer Weizman resigned from the Cabinet and Begin's coalition began to unravel. During his term as Minister of Agriculture, Sharon displayed a deep contempt and an aggressive disrespect toward his colleagues and terrorized all of them, including the Prime Minister. Begin, who was aging and increasingly prone to mood changes, was, contrary to his public image, a weak premier who was unable to discipline his ministers, especially Sharon. Although he resisted Sharon's effort to intimidate him after Weizman's resignation and refused to nominate him as Minister of Defense, the fall of his government, the impending elections, and the evacuation of Jewish settlements from the Sinai all made him realize how much he depended on Sharon. Begin appointed Sharon as the manager of the Likud electoral campaign, promising him that if Likud won the election, Sharon would be named Minister of Defense. This is, of course, what happened.

---

17 Indeed, Israel has always rejected the definition of the territories as occupied, claiming that they were never under the sovereignty of another state (since the annexation of the West Bank by Jordan was never recognized by the international community, with the exception of Britain and Pakistan), and because they maintain that the lands came under their control during a just and defensive war. Israel did, however, take it upon itself to abide by international law in the territories, including the Fourth Geneva Convention of 1949. However, most experts in the field of international law do not accept this approach. They are divided between seeing Israel as an occupying power and seeing Israel as a trustee-occupant—controlling the territory until the dormant sovereignty of the local residents, a distinct socio-political entity, develops into a self-ruling body.

10   The Second Attempt at Politicide

On August 5, 1981, Menachem Begin established his second and last government. It included Ariel Sharon as Minister of Defense. Sharon's first big mission was to implement the last stage of the Israeli–Egyptian peace accord, namely the dismantlement or, more accurately, the complete destruction, of all Jewish settlements in the Sinai. Gush Emunim tried to organize not only local resistance to evacuation, but also a countrywide mass movement close to civil rebellion in order to stop the withdrawal. The spiritual leaders of Gush Emunim (mainly rabbis) called on soldiers to disobey orders to implement the evacuation, and a group of zealots blockaded themselves in a bunker and threatened to commit suicide if forced to evacuate. The Gush tried to construct a sociopolitical reality of national trauma that would be carved in the collective memory forever, but they completely failed. Some of the settlers accepted the generous compensation that was offered by the government and financed by a special American aid package and left the settlements peacefully. Most of the outsiders who came to reinforce the local resistance were settlers from the West Bank who feared that the evacuation of the Sinai would serve as a precedent for their own eventual removal. However, under Sharon's direction, the April 1982 evacuation of the Sinai settlements took place in a few days and without any serious incidents.[18]

18 The movement's adherents and some settlers and psychologists argued that the uprooted settlers would suffer all their lives from "evacuation trauma," a trauma

One might ask how it was that a man who did more to develop the settlements than anyone, except perhaps Moshe Dayan, could manage their dismantlement in such a highly efficient way. His conduct was particularly surprising since, during the long years of negotiations between Egypt and Israel, Sharon had consistently opposed evacuation and had been the only Likud Knesset member who voted against the peace agreement. Furthermore, during his term as Minister of Agriculture (and later in Netanyahu's government as Minister of National Infrastructures), he had done everything possible to enlarge the settlements. Some detractors claim that Sharon's willingness to implement the evacuation reveals the hypocritical and selfish character of a man who is always eager to do anything to advance his interests. In his autobiography, Sharon dedicated many pages to describing the meaning and importance of the peace with Egypt. Benziman, in his biography, provides a third explanation, which is that Sharon became enthusiastic about the peace accord with Egypt only when he was personally involved and exclusively in charge of its implementation.

All these explanations may be true and are not necessarily mutually exclusive. However, Sharon's readiness to pay any price in order to remove Egypt from the game must be understood in terms of Begin and Sharon's geopolitical perception of the Israeli–Palestinian and regional conflicts, some of which have been described very well by Ze'ev Schiff and Ehud Ya'ari in their book *Israel's Lebanon War*.[19]

---

that never existed. For some, this psychological argument was used to support their ideology, for others it helped to maximize their material compensation.

19 Schiff, a veteran and highly respected (although conservative) military analyst of *Ha'aretz*, was the first to disclose Sharon's grand design of creating a new order in Lebanon several months before the invasion in a newspaper article in which he

Israel's consolidation of control over the West Bank and Gaza—especially after the Camp David Accords, where Begin committed himself to granting them full autonomy within five years—required the politicide of the Jewish state's only existential enemy. While the Arab states, according to this perception, were bitter but manageable enemies, only the stateless Palestinians could have a moral and historical claim against the entire Jewish entity established in 1948 on the ruins of their society.

After the re-politicization of the Palestinian refugee problem and its redefinition as an ethno-national issue following the 1973 War, and after the Palestinian refusal to adopt Sharon's equation of "Jordan is Palestine," only their politicide could, from Sharon's point of view, resolve the conflict. But the only way to implement this politicide without provoking a major regional war in which the Palestinians would collude with the attacking states was to make peace with the most powerful Arab country in the region.

The politicide of the Palestinians might include destroying their institutional and military infrastructure in southern Lebanon and possibly annihilating Fatah and other top PLO political and military organizations. This new political reality would, from this point of view, force Palestinians in the West Bank and Gaza Strip into accepting any solution dictated by the Israelis. To achieve this goal, the invasion of Lebanon and the support of an internal ally within the country were necessary. Moreover, Sharon's vision was larger. According to his perception, only the expulsion of Syrians from

---

warned about the implications. Some senior officers who tried to help Israel avoid the adventure probably leaked the plan to Schiff, but the disclosure did not help.

Lebanon and the establishment of a government that was friendly to Israel and would sign a peace agreement with her could change the geopolitical reality of the region. How little knowledge of Lebanon in particular, and sociopolitical processes in general, this power-oriented megalomaniac possessed can be easily discerned from this plan.

As a matter of fact, the Lebanese ally Sharon envisioned already existed: the Maronite Christian community. One of the earliest Zionist fantasies was the establishment in the region of an alliance of minorities (Christians, Jews, Druzes, Circassians, etc.) to counterbalance the Muslim majority of the region. Since the mid-1950s, the Maronite Christians of Lebanon had been involved in civil wars and violence resulting from their loss of hegemony in the country, a loss that was partially caused by a policy of territorial expansion that brought non-Maronite ethno-religious groups (Muslims and Druses) under their control. The latecomers were the Palestinian refugees of 1948, whom the Maronites blamed for the country's internal instability. However, it was only in the spring of 1976 that one of the Maronite factions, the Phalange Party, headed by Pierre Gemayel and his son Bashir, turned secretly to Israel for military aid in their struggle against the leftist Palestinian–Druze coalition headed by Kamal Jumblatt. During the negotiations, another Maronite leader, Danny Chamoun, exclaimed to an Israeli team, "Give us arms and we shall slaughter the Palestinians." This request was made during Rabin's first term and he cautiously refrained from any direct intervention, but shipments of arms and ammunition, including M-16 rifles, LOW antitank missiles, and some old Sherman tanks, were sent to Christian militias, with a liaison officer named Benjamin Ben Eliezer serving as a go-between. Israel developed a more direct and intimate relationship with the southern border villagers and with a local Christian militia headed by Major Sa'ad Haddad, an official appointee of the de facto nonexistent Lebanese Army. The collaboration was solidified and made public during Begin's first term. Begin was impressed by the pleas and the aristocratic manner of the Maronite leaders and several times declared "Israel will not allow genocide [of the Maronites] in Lebanon." In March 1978, Israeli forces temporarily occupied southern Lebanon, in an attempt to neutralize Palestinian guerilla groups and enlarge the territory controlled by Major Haddad, in an undertaking called Operation Litani (the river that more or less marked the boundary of the Israeli influence). The operation was abortive because the guerilla forces avoided fighting and fled to the north only to return after the Israeli withdrawal.

Soon afterwards, the Maronites decided that they preferred an alliance with the Syrians and invited them to enter the country and slaughter the Palestinian militia and civilians. But the Syrians soon changed sides after their local vassal, Tony Frangieh, was killed in a vendetta by Bashir Gemayel, and the Phalangists turned against the rival Christian militia. The Christians successfully tried to involve both the Israelis and, at the same time, the Syrians, whose military presence gradually increased.[20]

During this period, Israel nominated a new Chief of Staff—Rafael

---

20 In Lebanon, there were at least three different—and rival—Christian militias, each of them affiliated with one of the great patriarchal families. Israel invested a lot of energy trying to unify these militias and merge them together into a Lebanese army, but without success. Only after massacres committed by the militias against each other did Bashir Gemayel and his Phalangists manage to take over the other two militias, but not Haddad's, which was protected by Israel.

Eitan, who was well known for his limited intellectual horizons, his derogatory attitude toward Arabs, and his joy of battle. Prime Minister Begin, who also served during this period as Minister of Defense following Weizman's resignation, believed a war in Lebanon was necessary both because of the failure of Operation Litani and because of Syria's increasing military and political penetration into the country. In addition, the new election was looming and the Begin government's prospects looked bad. Thus, Begin, in collaboration with Eitan, made two major decisions in May of 1981: to destroy the Iraqi nuclear reactor and to inflame the northern border.[21] Between March 29 and July 3, 1981, Israel bombarded Palestinian targets in Lebanon by air and sea. The Palestinians refused to react, recognizing Israel's interest in escalating the conflict. On July 9, Israel renewed their attacks on Palestinian targets but this time, after a week of uninterrupted shelling, the Palestinians responded by targeting the Israeli coastal town of Nahariya with Katyusa rockets. Israel retaliated almost immediately, sending aircraft to destroy the command head-quarters of Fatah and the Democratic Front, which lay within a densely populated area of Beirut. Summarizing the results of the attack, Ze'ev Schiff and Ehud Ya'ari wrote that "the results [of the action] were predictable. Despite pains taken [by the pilots] to pinpoint the targets and achieve direct hits, over 100 people were killed and some 600 wounded; estimates in Israel were that only thirty of the dead were terrorists." Now the Palestinian response was

---

21 Since Ben-Gurion's period, Israeli politicians have known that the best way to divert public attention away from economic and other domestic difficulties is to focus on the Jewish–Arab conflict.

merciless: with field artillery and rockets, they paralyzed life in northern Israel, including the towns of Kiryat Shmone and Nahariya, for ten days, causing a partial evacuation of the population from the area. In spite of overwhelming military superiority, the Israeli field artillery and bombardiers were unable to silence the light and highly mobile Palestinian guerilla artillery. When the American envoy Philip Habib arrived in the region to negotiate between Israel and the PLO, Begin agreed to a truce on July 24. This was the first indirect agreement between Israel and the PLO and was strictly observed by both sides.

It is not clear, even today, to what extent Begin was a knowing and full partner in Ariel Sharon's grand design and if Sharon deceived him about his ultimate aims when he convinced him to initiate the war in Lebanon (the issue was even the subject of two libel suits brought by Sharon himself against *Ha'aretz* and *Time* magazine when they accused him of misleading Begin and hiding the ultimate aims of the invasion from him). However, a careful reading of the historical record seems not to support this allegation. What is clear is that the Israeli Cabinet never directly approved of either the operation or its political goals. The ministers were asked to approve the operation piece by piece and mostly retroactively. For example, the crucial decision to take over the highway between Beirut and Damascus was put on the Cabinet's agenda in the context of a possible Syrian military response to the annexation of the Golan Heights by Israel in December 1981. Other decisions were made under pressure when battlefield conditions were changing rapidly and after Sharon had manipulated the Cabinet, a skill he developed into an art form during his active military career, using false reports about the battlefield and taking advantage of the Cabinet members' inability to read military maps.

Begin understood and was in full agreement with Sharon about the necessity of expelling the PLO from Lebanon as well as about the dangers of becoming involved in a partial or full-scale war. He probably knew about the plans to establish a new regime in Lebanon at bayonet point and about the intensive negotiations between Israeli delegations and all the echelons and factions of the Maronites. At the same time, American Secretary of State Alexander Haig toured the region and left Begin and his government with the impression that the United States viewed Syria as a Soviet satellite and would allow Israel to adopt a hard-line policy toward it. In the meantime, the commander of the southern front, General Amir Drori was instructed to prepare detailed plans for the various stages of an invasion of Lebanon (Operation Small Pines was the code name for the minimalist version of the operation and Operation Grand Pines for the large-scale one).

The Egyptian intelligence service, and probably others as well, leaked Israel's invasion plans to the Palestinians and must also have given some details to the Syrians. The Palestinian leadership decided not to give Israel any pretext to attack. Moreover, according to Schiff and Ya'ari, a despairing Yasser Arafat sent Begin a personal message through a United Nations envoy: "I have learned more from you as a resistance leader than anyone else about how to combine politics with military tactics . . . You of all people must understand that it is not necessary to face me only on the battlefield. Do not send a military force against me. Do not try to break me in Lebanon. You will not succeed." The message went unanswered.

On the evening of June 3, 1982, Israel's ambassador in London was shot and badly wounded by a hit squad sent by Abu Nidal from Damascus. Since the mini-state resolution of the Palestinian National Council of July 1974, Abu Nidal had broken with the PLO, had called Arafat a traitor, and had tried several times to assassinate him. Arafat responded by sentencing him to death. Abu Nidal's action was, as Israeli intelligence services knew very well, a deliberate provocation. However, when the Israeli Cabinet gathered the next morning, this information was intentionally withheld by the Prime Minister (Sharon, as Minister of Defense, was on a secret journey but returned immediately afterwards on the same day). Begin depicted the assassination attempt as a declaration of war and a deliberate repudiation of Habib's truce agreement with the PLO. On that Friday, the Cabinet decided to send the air force to bombard "terrorist headquarters" in Beirut. The Palestinians retaliated promptly by shelling northern Israel. That Saturday evening, a Cabinet meeting was held in Begin's home where the Prime Minister and the Minister of Defense unveiled the details of a military operation to protect Israel's northern settlements from terrorist artillery by creating a buffer zone that would extend forty kilometers north of Israel's border. Further goals of the operation included an avoidance of conflict with Syrian troops stationed in Lebanon and the establishment of a stable peace with a free and sovereign Lebanon. This was a cunning definition of the operation's aims (Begin, when speaking the next day before the Knesset, called the plan Operation Peace for Galilee). Sharon asserted later that the Cabinet had approved his whole plan, while the ministers, who later denied any responsibility for the war, argued that the resolution for making peace was not intended as an order for a military operation but a general declaration of being in a state of peace with a neighboring country. In any case, before the Cabinet had even met, elite Israeli units were landing far north of the specified forty-kilometer line.[22]

Aware of the criticism leveled against him by the Cabinet and by Begin himself, Sharon stated in his autobiography that, contrary to the habit of the previous Ministers of Defense, he determined "that the political echelon would maintain [in that war] firm control over the battlefield. As a result, I made sure that the Cabinet was informed of every significant development and potential development. I saw to it that every decision was made in the Cabinet and that the orders issued to the army had been decided upon by them." In one assertion, Sharon is right. Previous defense ministers never asked cabinets for confirmation of every move made during battle. However, unlike Sharon, no previous Minister of Defense ever initiated such an adventurous war.

Seemingly from the start, the military calculations went wrong. The original estimated time for arrival in the Beirut region was about three days. However, the Israeli forces met far more stubborn Palestinian resistance than was expected (these battles gave birth to the "RPG-kids" legend about the young Palestinians who faced Israeli armor) and were engaged by Syrian troops that attacked Israeli units (following Israeli provocations) and inflicted considerable casualties.

22 The majority of the opposition Labor Party's leadership was composed of ex-generals (Yitzhak Rabin, Haim Bar-Lev, Mordechai Gur, etc.) or men who were formerly part and parcel of the security establishment, like Shimon Peres, and they maintained an old-boy network of relationships with the military high command. So, presumably, they were more up-to-date on the military plans and intentions and understood them much better than most of the cabinet ministers. They also continued to support the war as long as there was no popular protest.

The first ground battles with the Palestinians were in the Tyre-Sidon area, where seven major refugee camps—al-Bass, al-Hanina, Rashidiyah, Beni Mashouq, Burj al-Shemali, Ain al-Hilweh and Sha-briqa—were located. The Palestinians employed the classic guerilla war strategy of hit-and-run attacks by small and mobile units. The large quasi-regular brigades (such as al-Kastel or Karameh) were almost never used. From the very first days of the war, the Palestinians delayed the expected Israeli blitzkrieg on Beirut, exposing Israeli forces to strong resistance by blocking the roads going north and inflicting many casualties. At the al-Bass crossroad, within Ain al-Hilweh, that held out until June 17 and was called the "Palestinian Stalingrad," and later on at the battle over the Beaufort fortress,[23] the Palestinians succeeded in halting Israeli columns. Both battles became a story of heroism on both sides. The passage to the Sidon region took about forty-eight hours instead of the few hours planned, and Palestinian resistance was broken only after merciless and indiscriminate air bombardments. After the war, Israeli analysts concluded that most of the Palestinian leaders at the field-command level were below standard while the ability and motivation of the privates were high.

On June 11, a ceasefire was declared but Israeli forces continued

23 The Beaufort was a Crusader castle hewn in rock about 2,200 feet above sea level. It overlooked the territories of the Upper Galilee in Israel and the central part of southern Lebanon and was used to shell Israeli territory. The Israeli air force tried many times to destroy the fortress, but failed. An Israeli commando unit succeeded in taking over the fortress after heavy fighting in which all eighteen Palestinian defenders were killed. After the battle, Begin and Sharon arrived at Beaufort for a photo opportunity and Begin declared that the fortress was conquered without any Israeli casualties. In his autobiography, Sharon accused Rafael Eitan of feeding Begin this disinformation.

advancing toward Beirut. Another problem arose when Sharon discovered that Bashir Gemayel and his Phalangists did not want to take
over West (Muslim and Palestinian) Beirut, but expected Israeli
soldiers to do it for them. Their only contribution in the war "to
liberate Lebanon from the terrorists" was their capture, on June 16,
of the Faculty of Science building in the Reihan quarter, an action
that somewhat contributed to the Israeli effort to dominate West
Beirut. In fact, from the beginning, the Maronites were ambivalent
about their alliance with the Israelis. On the one hand, they needed
Israeli support to fight the perceived existential threat to their survival
as a community in Lebanon. On the other hand, they wanted to
continue to be considered as a part of the Arab world and culture,
and in this context, their alliance with Israel was considered
treasonous.

The Phalangist refusal to take West Beirut led Ariel Sharon to
besiege the city and demand the complete evacuation of PLO forces
and leaders. On June 25, Israeli troops finally conquered the Bham-
doun-Aley region, the presidential palace of Ba'abda, and the Beirut
international airport. At this stage, the commanders of two paratrooper brigades that were assigned to take over the city tried to
convince Sharon and Eitan that this move was mad, that it would
result in many casualties on both sides, and that it was simply
impossible to impose Maronite rule and Bashir Gemayel's presidency
on Lebanon. Gemayel will be assassinated just like King Abdullah and
Anwar Sadat, warned the two officers. When Sharon and Eitan
rejected the officers' arguments, one of them, Colonel Eli Geva,
announced to the Chief of Staff that he would refuse to give such an
order to his soldiers, but would instead fight alongside his soldiers as

a private. Sharon fired Geva immediately and rejected the request for leave of another officer, General Amram Mitzna.

Throughout this period, American envoys Philip Habib and Morris Draper tried to reach an agreement to end the war, proposing the evacuation of the PLO's guerilla forces and headquarters from the country, the stationing of international forces, and the withdrawal of Israeli troops. Besieged Beirut was under heavy and indiscriminate bombardment for weeks by Israeli artillery, armor, and air power, which reached its peak on August 12 (Black Thursday), one day after the Israeli Cabinet accepted Philip Habib's agreement for the PLO's evacuation from Lebanon. Israel launched a seven-hour uninterrupted raid on the city that claimed 300, mostly civilian, lives—this in a city whose main areas were already ruined, whose electricity and water supplies had been cut, and whose population was facing famine and an outbreak of epidemic diseases from the thousands of unburied corpses. This bombardment resembled the attack on Dresden by the Allies toward the end of World War II. On the same day, Sharon called up an additional paratrooper brigade. According to Benziman, when Sharon was asked by the Cabinet why he wanted to activate them, he enumerated two reasons: to save the lives of Israeli soldiers, and to persuade the PLO to accept Habib's terms. In fact, it seems that Sharon was interested, not in the evacuation of the PLO from Beirut, but in close combat that would lead to their physical annihilation. This time, even Begin was mad at his Defense Minister, who clearly intended to sabotage Habib's efforts to evacuate the PLO from Lebanon.

Finally, on August 13, an agreement was reached following pressure from the United States and its envoys Habib and Draper, contrary to Ariel Sharon's desires and plans. On the first day of

September, the last ships carrying Palestinian fighters (equipped only with light arms) left Beirut and other parts of Lebanon on their way to Tunis and Yemen. Before they left, Arafat asked that multinational forces be brought in to protect the Palestinians from Phalangist revenge. Sharon rejected the request, arguing that what the Palestinians really wanted was to avoid the collection of arms hidden in their camps and neighborhoods.

11   The Horror of Sabra and Shatila

On August 27, the Lebanese Parliament, under the "protection" of Israeli armed forces, elected Bashir Gemayel President of Lebanon. It seemed that Sharon's grand design was going to be accomplished and that he could enjoy a grand political victory, even if it was at the awful cost of thousands of dead and the destruction of West Beirut, one of the most vital and developed capitals of the Arab world.

Estimates of the total casualties suffered by Palestinian guerillas, Palestinian and Lebanese civilians, and Syrian military personnel are only approximate, but they are in the thousands. According to Robert Fisk, during the first three months of the invasion, about eighteen thousand people were killed throughout the occupied area, while in West Beirut alone about 2,500 were killed by air strikes, artillery, and naval gunfire. When the operation began, Menachem Begin estimated that at most there would be twenty-five Israeli casualties. On June 14, Chief of Staff Rafael Eitan announced that there were 170 dead and 700 wounded, but three days later the number jumped to 214 dead and 1,115 wounded. By 1985, when the major withdrawals began, Israel had more than a thousand dead in the war that was labeled Israel's Vietnam.

The received wisdom is that Menachem Begin left political life and fell into depression when he became aware of how badly Sharon had deceived him, but it seems more likely that, except in a few cases— like the air force's massive raid on Beirut—Begin had full knowledge of at least the broad outlines of Operation Grand Pines. In any case, he bears the full legal, moral, and political responsibility for the war no less than Sharon does. Begin's withdrawal from political life was caused precisely by the failure and high cost of a war that had been fought, not in self-defense, but to achieve political goals, a war that he had chosen to support with all the authority and moral leadership that his position as Prime Minister gave him.

Despite repeated efforts by Sharon, the politicide of the Palestinians was not yet complete, but they had suffered a major military, political and moral defeat. Arafat's only achievement, besides his success in saving most of the PLO combatants and their leadership, was the fourth article of the Habib–Draper document that was supposed to secure the safety of "law-abiding and non-combatant Palestinians who remain in Beirut," although it was not clear who was responsible for guaranteeing their safety.

But it was too early for Sharon to claim victory. Exactly as some of Sharon's officers expected, on September 14, 1982 at 4:30 pm, a Syrian agent blew up a powerful explosive device in the Phalanges' Ashrafiya headquarters, killing Bashir Gemayel. At that moment, the entire carefully planned operation collapsed like a house of cards and Sharon lost control over subsequent developments; but his personal fall began only after the world became aware of the dreadful massacres in Sabra and Shatila.

On the evening of September 16, one of the Phalangist's elite units, headed by the chief intelligence officer of the Christian militia, Allies Houbeika, and in cooperation with Israeli military forces, entered the Palestinian refugee camps of Sabra and Shatila (in fact, part of Beirut). During the next forty hours, they slaughtered between 700 and 2,000 men, women, and children while beating and raping others.[24] While the Phalangists were in the camps, they made an effort to bury the corpses in mass graves with bulldozers. The massacre was committed in a highly professional way, by militiamen moving in relative quiet from home to home so that the inhabitants were not alerted and not able to flee or resist (the exception being a light exchange of fire with some Palestinian youngsters when the Maronites first entered Shatila). During this time, Israeli forces sealed the camps, and a nearby Israeli military outpost which had not been informed of what was going to take place did not detect anything unusual, although some suspicions were raised and even reported to senior officers.

Accepted wisdom regards the massacre as a spontaneous reaction (revenge, so to speak) to the assassination of Bashir Gemayel two days earlier, but this is a simplistic attempt to explain and even excuse this horrifying event. The massacre, when seen in its proper political context, is even more dreadful. Following the departure of the PLO

24 The Israeli committee of inquiry (the Kahan Commission) accepted the figures offered by the Israeli intelligence services, which estimated a death toll of 700–800 people. The Palestinian Red Crescent put the death toll at 2,000, while the Lebanese authorities issued 1,200 death certificates for the victims.

and the Syrians from West Beirut and its Muslim neighborhoods, a question arose as to who was to take over these areas and how, since it was assumed that a lot of "terrorist" weapons and ammunition remained there. The Israelis preferred Christian troops like the almost nonexistent Lebanese Army. In Sharon's words:

> We [the Israelis] did not want our own soldiers taking casualties in street fighting, and the business of going after terrorists could be handled much more effectively by Arabic-speaking Lebanese familiar with the local accents and with the PLO's urban *modus operandi*. Lebanese troops, then, would be asked to move into West Beirut in conjunction with the IDF [Israel Defense Forces]. It would be their job to penetrate the neighborhoods and clean out the terrorists.

The second best choice was the Phalangists, and throughout the invasion, Israel made efforts to merge these two Christian "armies" (and other Christian militias) without success. In any case, both Christian military organizations wanted to see Beirut and all of Lebanon cleared of "terrorists," namely Palestinians, but they demanded that Israel do the job. In fact, the Christian Lebanese openly blamed Israel for all their troubles with the Palestinians, seeing the Zionists as responsible for the uprooting of the Palestinians in 1948 and their subsequent flight to Lebanon.

When Sharon urged the Phalangists to enter West Beirut, contrary to his testimony before the Kahan Commission, he was well aware of the atrocious past and present tendencies of the militia, having been warned several times by his intelligence and other officers and even by his colleagues in the Cabinet. One must also keep in mind that in inter-communal wars and conflicts, massacres and other atrocities committed against non-combatant populations are not just consequences of hatred and emotional outbursts, but also the results of calculated actions designed to force a population to flee to other lands and to ethnically cleanse an area without the difficult logistical problems of a forced evacuation.[25] The Maronite community never hid their desire to expel the Palestinians from the country. Their only problem was where the Palestinians should go: neither Syria nor Jordan (nor of course, Israel) would welcome them. In addition, even their removal from the Beirut region to a more peripheral area would be only a partial victory for the Maronites. There was also some conflict of interest between the Israelis and the Maronites. Schiff and Ya'ari report that, in the first phases of the invasion, one of Begin's and Sharon's goals was to push the Palestinian inhabitants of southern Lebanon—not only the combatants—to the north, and for this reason, as many houses as possible were destroyed by Israel's artillery and air force and measures were taken to prevent their being rebuilt. But this policy was not pursued for long because it was blatantly opposed to the interests of Israel's supposed ally.

After the massacre, the Israeli Government tried to diminish its significance and gravity and to downplay its own responsibility, hoping that domestic and international indignation would soon be abated. The insensitivity and ethnocentric nature of its approach were demonstrated by Begin's famous pronouncement, "Gentiles kill gentiles and then accuse the Jews"—so, what do Jews have to do with it? But

---

25 Thus, Begin in his book *The Revolt* boasted that the action of his paramilitary organization Etzel in Deir Yassin encouraged the flight of Arabs from the country.

the public furor was enormous. On September 25, about 400,000 angry demonstrators gathered in Tel Aviv's central square demanding an independent commission of inquiry. Prominent public figures, intellectuals, and scientists also demanded an inquiry into the event and the resignation of those responsible for the massacre. After ten tense days, Begin nominated a commission of inquiry presided over by Chief Justice Yitzhak Kahan.

In fact, the unprecedented public anger over the massacre was the culmination of a growing uneasiness about the whole war, both at the front lines and at home. The soldiers knew about the increasing discrepancies between what they actually did, the disinformation of the military spokesmen, and the declarations of the Prime Minister and Minister of Defense. Additionally, they were less able than ever to understand the logic behind the military operation. For the first time in Israeli history, the phenomenon of conscientious objection appeared as soldiers refused to serve on Lebanese soil. The next time this phenomenon was to occur in Israel, it would be linked again to one of Sharon's attempts to commit politicide against the Palestinians.

Mistrust of the government and its policies grew rapidly. After the assassination attempt on ambassador Argov, the sensational publicity following it, and the shelling of towns in northern Israel, the public and the opposition political parties had largely supported Operation Peace for the Galilee during its initial stages. As long as the war seemed to be successful and casualties low, public support continued. But once the increasingly high casualty figures became public, the discrepancies between the initial goal of creating a buffer zone for the northern region and the actual conduct of the war became a major public issue and a cause of civil unrest.

Other players in this game included the different factions operating
in Lebanon and the international community. Arafat pleaded repeatedly but in vain for Syria to help him. The Syrians conducted heavy
battles with Israeli forces only when they were directly threatened.
The invasion of Lebanon was begun immediately following the
annexation of the Golan Heights and the Syrian suspicion seemed to
be that both Israeli moves were intended to provoke a war against
Syria and Hafez Assad's regime, and they didn't want to provide any
pretext for the Israelis.[26] The other Lebanese militias regarded the
Palestinians as rivals and turned against Israel only after it prolonged
its presence there. The Soviets and some European countries
expressed sympathy but were totally helpless to provide diplomatic
or military support to Lebanon. The major external player was, of
course, the United States under Ronald Reagan. The US administration had a double commitment to two difficult allies: Saudi Arabia
and Israel. The Saudis were never great fans of the PLO and Arafat,
but in the face of Israel's invasion, they felt an obligation to intervene
by using their influence in the US. From the start, Washington made
it clear to the Israelis that the attack on ambassador Argov did not
justify a full-scale invasion, although Secretary of State Alexander
Haig, a former general and a very hawkish man, found common
ground with Sharon and gave him and the Israeli Government the
impression that the Reagan administration would tolerate a short and

---

26 Begin and Sharon, facing the messy situation in Lebanon, contemplated
sharing control or influence over the country between Israel and Syria. The southern
part of the country would be under Israeli control, while the northern part would be
under Syrian control. De facto, this was indeed the situation between 1985 and
2000, when Ehud Barak finally withdrew Israeli troops from Lebanon.

"clean military operation" (i.e., without unnecessary casualties) in Lebanon. Haig was so sympathetic to the Israelis that several times he promised them more than the Reagan administration was willing to provide and was obliged to issue clarifications that were really withdrawals of his initial positions and promises. Finally, he was obliged to quit and was replaced by George Shultz. The tension between the United States and Israel began earlier, when Israel annexed the Golan Heights. In response, the US suspended the much-desired Memorandum of Strategic Understanding—a low-level military pact that had recently been signed by Sharon and Secretary of Defense Caspar Weinberger. Seemingly, Washington never did develop a clear policy toward the invasion. The US ambassador in Tel Aviv, Samuel Lewis, had a series of difficult conversations with Begin. Begin accused him of trying to interfere in Israeli politics and Lewis, not very diplomatically, accused Begin and Sharon of deceiving the American administration. In the field, Philip Habib and Morris Draper performed admirably. In fact, Sharon faced only two major constraints that curbed him in some measure and prevented him from fully implementing his grand design—American pressure and Israeli public opinion, which was clearly influenced not only by the horror of Sabra and Shatila, but also by the heavy casualties and by the sense that the government had violated an unwritten social contract that the military, which was largely staffed by reserve soldiers, could only be used for consensual wars. Sharon learned this lesson well, as will be demonstrated later in the discussion of his political comeback in 2000.

On February 9, 1983, the Kahan Commission's report was published: some senior military officers (including the Chief of Staff and the head of military intelligence) were found negligent in fulfilling their roles, and it was recommended that some of them be dismissed. The commission concluded that the Prime Minister, although not directly involved in the affair, still had some degree of overall responsibility, but no specific recommendation was made regarding him.

In fact, the US administration shares much of the indirect responsibility for the massacre. The PLO negotiators were well aware of the danger of leaving the civilian Palestinian population unprotected. They were ready, after forty days of siege, to leave Beirut, but demanded firm guarantees from the US. On August 20, the US sent a memorandum to the PLO, including the following commitment: "Law-abiding Palestinian non-combatants remaining in Beirut, including the families of those who have departed, will be authorized to live in peace and security. . . . The US will provide its guarantee on the basis of assurances received from the Government of Israel and from other leaders of certain Lebanese groups [i.e., the Phalanges and the Lebanese army] with which it [the US] has been in contact." The well-known Palestinian historian Rashid Khalidi, who wrote a book about the PLO decision-making process during the war, raised another interesting question about the PLO leadership's responsibility for the massacre. He emphasized the complete isolation of the Palestinians from any potential supporters including Arabs and other major powers and the opinion at the time that continuing the battle would lead to the complete destruction of Beirut and the enormous suffering of all the inhabitants of Lebanon. Khalidi concluded that "it is difficult to see how a responsible political leadership could have made any choice other than the one they did [to evacuate], cruel though its results proved to be in the end." Anyway, the Kahan Commission found that Sharon bore a major part of the responsibility for the massacre:

According to our best judgment, responsibility is to be imputed to the Minister of Defense for having disregarded the prospect of acts of revenge and bloodshed by the Phalangists against the population of the refugee camps and for having failed to take this danger into consideration. . . . We believe that the Minister of Defense bears personal responsibility . . . [and] it is appropriate that the Minister of Defense draw the proper personal conclusions regarding the faults revealed in the manner in which he discharged the duties of his office and if necessary that the Prime Minister should consider exercising his authority accordingly . . . [and] after informing the Cabinet of the intention to do so, remove the Minister [of Defense] from office.

Ariel Sharon—after the findings and unequivocal conclusions of the Kahan Commission of Inquiry—was considered to be political dead wood from a moral and even a legal point of view. However, in accordance with its letter of appointment, the Kahan Commission inquired only into the localized affair of Sabra and Shatila and did not examine the event within its wider context of the Israeli invasion of Lebanon and the political reasons and human consequences of this war. If such an inquiry had been made, a wide spectrum of the Israeli political and military leadership would have been found to be, at least from a moral point of view, war criminals, guilty not only of crimes against the Palestinians and the Lebanese but also against the Jewish people of Israel.

PART II

THE ROAD TO SHARONISM

12   From Civil Rebellion to Inter-Communal War

To understand both the present situation in the Holy Land and its various possible outcomes, it is necessary to briefly survey four pivotal events that occurred before Ariel Sharon's landslide victories in the 2001 and 2003 elections. These events are the first Intifada, the Oslo Accords, the abortive negotiations between Ehud Barak and Yasser Arafat at Camp David under the auspices of Bill Clinton, and the earlier stages of the current al-Aqsa Intifada. The major aim of the second part of this volume is to provide insights into the underlying reasons for two dramatic and contradictory shifts in the Israeli–Palestinian relationship—namely, the first major attempt at reconciliation and its collapse into a bloody inter-communal war that has greatly distorted and critically damaged both societies, albeit in different ways, and whose end is not yet in sight.

On December 9, 1987, an event occurred that was both predictable and unexpected. After twenty years of quiescence, a general popular uprising against the occupation erupted in the Gaza Strip and spread to the West Bank. The PLO leadership outside the territories was no less surprised than the Israelis. This revolt, later known as the Intifada, started as a spontaneous outburst but later became well coordinated. Local and country-wide clandestine popular committees were formed and the so-called Unified Leadership of the Revolt, operating inside the territories, gave directives to the local population. These directives, which were formally ratified by the PLO leadership outside, were spread mainly by leaflets (bayans). One result of the Intifada was that, for the first time since 1948, political power within the Palestinian community shifted away from leaders in exile to the still young and faceless leaders inside the country.

This was a genuine popular revolt, whose manifestations included mass demonstrations in the towns and camps, strikes, the waving of the banned Palestinian flag, and stone-throwing by youngsters, some of them women, who targeted Israeli forces operating inside the occupied territories. Thus, the image of the RPG-kids was supplanted by the image of the "stone-kids." It was also the beginning of the shuhada phenomenon, in which young men killed during the uprising were termed shahids (martyrs—a word carrying both religious and secular-nationalist connotations). Occasionally, individual Jewish civilians and soldiers were stabbed, mainly by young women armed with knives. Sometimes, Molotov cocktails were thrown. The Israeli military, helpless in the face of this kind of resistance, used tear gas, truncheons, and later rubber bullets to try to scatter the demonstrators.[1]

---

1 Rubber bullets are live ammunition. They are bullets wrapped in rubber or plastic that softens their impact and results in fewer fatalities. However, this "soft" ammunition killed some Palestinians and left many others maimed for life.

With few exceptions, the Palestinians avoided classic guerilla tactics and terrorist activities and succeeded in greatly neutralizing Israel's vast military superiority while using the local and foreign media to bring their message of an uncompromising demand for freedom to the world.

Yitzhak Rabin, the Minister of Defense in the National Unity Government, tried to suffocate the revolt by resorting to brutal physical violence but without using firearms. He ordered his soldiers to beat Palestinian stone-throwers, to break their legs or arms, and to detain thousands in camps without trial by using administrative detentions. The Israeli–Palestinian confrontation took a curious turn, being fought, at the end of the second millennium, with stones and clubs. However, Rabin, a soldier, drew two major conclusions from the Palestinian rebellion and the Israeli response. One was that the prolonged occupation was harmful to the Israeli armed forces and to Israeli security in strategic terms. Instead of being a military force trained to fight wars with the most modern and sophisticated military equipment, the Israeli military was in danger of becoming a police force that was losing its ability to fight real wars. Finite military resources were used to protect dozens of small settlements, their roads, and the buses carrying settler children to schools. Additionally, the army was called on to protect Palestinians from vigilante settlers. Rabin concluded that this situation not only wasted valuable human resources but undermined the proper military mentality because soldiers were being promoted not for their skill in combat, but for their merits as policemen. Rabin's other conclusion from his period as Minister of Defense, in sharp contradiction to Sharon's conclusions five years later, was that there is no military solution to the Israeli–

Palestinian conflict. But Rabin, like Sharon, distrusted Arabs in general and Palestinians in particular. Rabin's overall conclusions and complex worldview became, to a large degree, a basis for decisive action when he was elected Prime Minister five years later.

13   Oslo

Following the 1992 election, a minority coalition headed by the Labor Party and Yitzhak Rabin returned to power. Labor had joined forces with the center-left Meretz, and this minority coalition was able to form a stable government only with the support of two additional small parties associated with Arab voters and communists.[2] Nevertheless, it was large enough to block the formation of a rightwing coalition.

Although the Labor Party's electoral platform had promised to solve the Palestinian problem, the party had no clear plan for doing so. In contrast to Labor's traditional opposition to the formation of a Palestinian state alongside Israel, most of Meretz and the two supporting parties generally favored the establishment of such an entity.

As already stated, Rabin himself had reached the conclusion that there could be no military solution to the Palestinian uprising. Hence,

2 Meretz itself is a combination of three parties centered around the Human Rights Party, founded by Shulamit Aloni. Shas, the traditionalist party of Mizrahim, Jews who immigrated into Israel from Muslim Lands, was supposed to join the coalition, but after their political leader, Aryeh Deri, had legal difficulties, the party remained outside the coalition.

he reacted seriously and sympathetically when a proposal for talks between Israeli academics and some mid-level PLO officials was brought before him. These talks, which were to be held under the auspices of the Norwegian Government and its Foreign Minister Yohan Jurgen Holst, received retrospective authorization from the Israeli Foreign Minister Shimon Peres, and Vice Foreign Minister Yossi Beilin continued the negotiations, albeit secretly, once official sanction had been granted. The moment Palestinians signaled their readiness for an interim agreement, the Israeli Government began examining options. Shortly before this, the idea of withdrawing from the Gaza Strip, an area that was densely populated, difficult to control, and devoid of resources, had already become widespread among Israeli policy makers and some rightwing politicians. The difficulty was in finding an orgaization that was willing to assume responsibility and control of the Gaza Strip without demanding a comprehensive withdrawal from all the occupied territories.

According to the record of the unofficial talks in Norway, it became apparent that the PLO was ready to take responsibility for the Gaza Strip and an additional symbolic part of the West Bank without insisting on the prior negotiation of a detailed final-status agreement. This readiness was supposed to be part of an agreement that would be implemented in stages and that included the establishment of a Palestinian National Authority (PNA) in the West Bank and Gaza Strip and the eventual transfer of substantial parts of the occupied territories to sole control by the PLO.

In August 1993, this agreement became official and led to the signing of the Declaration of Principles (DOP) in Washington DC on September 13. The first stage outlined in the DOP obliged Israel to turn over most of the Gaza Strip (with the exception of the Jewish settlements in the Katif bloc—composed of some hundred families occupying about a quarter of the most densely populated area in the world) and the Jericho area (according to the Cairo Agreement of May 4, 1994) to the newly established Palestinian National Authority. In the following stages, the PNA was supposed to gain sole control over all Palestinian cities and the highly populated refugee camps in the West Bank and Gaza Strip (with the exception of settled Jewish areas in the city of Hebron). The total territory to be transferred to sole Palestinian control (Area A) was about 4 percent of the West Bank and Gaza Strip. Also agreed upon was an intermediary division of the rest of the territory of the West Bank and Gaza Strip into two areas of control. The area under sole Israeli control encompassed the Jordan Valley, all the Jewish settlements in the West Bank, and their avenues of access (Area C), while the area of joint control encompassed most of the rural areas of the West Bank, including about 440 villages and the surrounding lands (Area B). In Area B, the Palestinian authority was to have control over administrative issues and Israel was to retain authority over military issues; joint Israeli–Palestinian patrols were also agreed upon (Area B).

Working under the assumption that taking things a step at a time would build trust, the agreement intended to transfer incrementally the entire Palestinian population of the West Bank and Gaza Strip (with the exception of East Jerusalem and the surrounding metropolitan area) to Palestinian control. The Jewish settlements in the occupied territories (including access roads) and their populations would remain under Israeli control.

This interim agreement was supposed to last five years, during which time a final agreement would be reached on a myriad of issues, including the status of East Jerusalem, borders, the refugee problem, the final status of the PNA, the division of water in the common aquifer, and the use of airspace.

The Israelis were also obliged to grant free and secure passage between the two parts of the PNA's territory, to release prisoners and captives, and to grant aid (together with the United States and the European countries) for projects, like an international airport and a deep-water port in Gaza, whose purpose was to develop the economic and social infrastructure in areas under PNA control. In exchange, the only thing the Palestinians promised, besides the recognition of Israel, was an end to the guerilla warfare against Israel and an active campaign to prevent terrorist acts against Israel, Israelis, and even residents of the Jewish settlements in the occupied territories. For this purpose, the establishment of a Palestinian police force and various types of security forces (such as the Preventive Security forces) was agreed upon.

The PNA itself was interested in the establishment of these militia units for several reasons. The establishment of a Palestinian police force made it possible for a large portion of the paramilitary units (and their families) who had been deported from Lebanon to Tunis to return to Palestine. Other units of the Palestine Liberation Army that had been dispersed among several other countries were also permitted to return. These latter units, together with local forces (mostly Fatah veterans), were integrated with the units brought from Tunis and became the main force on which the PNA regime, which saw itself as a state in the making, could depend. Today these units are perceived as the Old Guard, as opposed to the local Young Guard.

These organizations were part of a large bureaucratic mechanism—a frequent characteristic of non-industrial, developing states. In the absence of productive economic infrastructures, these mechanisms serve an additional function beyond the advancement of their overt institutional aims. As a source of employment and income for a wide stratum of the population, they promote the legitimate inflow of cash resources and act to preserve loyalties to the regime. The "Palestinian army," with its uniforms and weapons (from light to mid-range), created a satisfying and necessary national symbol for the Palestinians. According to the agreement, the branches of this militia could total 9,000 men, but in reality their numbers quickly surpassed that figure. Later, and mostly due to the increase in armed rebellion and terrorist activities against Israel beginning in October 2000, the lines between the official militias and various other armed groups with varying degrees of support and control by the PNA blurred considerably. The best known of these local, quasi-official militias was the Fatah-Tanzim, or the "Organization," which was composed of young locals—as opposed to the veterans brought from Tunis—who declared their personal loyalty to Fatah, the PNA, and Arafat. They saw themselves both as an internal security organization that supplemented the ineffective blue police and as a force that could be turned against Israel if need be.

The Palestinian people themselves were divided on the very recognition of Israel as well as on the nature of the interim agreements that were to bring about the formation of the PNA. Even among the founders of Fatah itself—not to mention members of the Democratic Front, the Popular Front, and the Islamic Movement—there were those who completely rejected the agreement. They saw the Fatah leadership's agreement to establish the PNA, and perhaps later a dependent and demilitarized state on a torn and divided territory comprising only a miniscule part of historical (British) Palestine, as a disaster and an act of treason. Major opposition to the agreement came from Palestinians in exile, who felt that the PLO leadership had abandoned them by surrendering their right of return. They adhered to the central tenet of the Palestinian diaspora—that the right of return is the basic right of both each individual and the community which had been ripped from its homeland by force.

Perhaps the best-known opponent of the agreement was Edward Said, a fierce critic of the "orientalist" approach in Western culture. Said, who supported the PLO and Arafat and who is generally considered a moderate, came out immediately against the DOP and viewed the arrangement as a total surrender to Zionism and the West. According to this view, Israel had applied the classic colonial strategy that tries to convert *direct* military control into *indirect* control by taking advantage of Palestinian collaborators and utilizing its economic, technological, and military superiority.

Other Palestinian critics of the agreement, mostly "internal" people, who had spent most of their life under Israeli occupation (like the Gazanian political activist Dr. Haidar Abed al-Shafi and Mahmmud Darwish, who is considered the Palestinian national poet), were willing to agree to the principles of the peace agreement with Israel and to recognize the state, but criticized the conditions under which Arafat and the mainstream leadership were willing to accept them. These conditions seemed completely unsatisfactory and raised doubts as to the Israelis' true intentions. These opponents protested against, among other things, leaving Jewish settlements in the Palestinian territories (mostly in the heart of Hebron and the Gaza Strip) during the interim period, the postponement of the final-status talks over Jerusalem, the delayed release of Palestinian prisoners, and the small amount of territory to be transferred to the PNA.

13   The Establishment of the Palestinian National Authority

Arafat and his supporters endangered their political positions, and maybe even their lives, by agreeing to the Israeli conditions, which they themselves considered draconian. They were, however, mostly focused on the final arrangement through which the Palestinians would supposedly win an independent and sovereign state for the first time in history. This state was supposed to cover most of the territory of the West Bank and Gaza Strip, with East Jerusalem as its capital, and would include only a small minority of Jewish settlers and settlements within its borders. It was to pass its own Law of Return and to encourage selectively the migration of Palestinians from the diaspora to the new state, according to its economic ability for absorption, its ideological needs, and the pace it saw fit to set.

When the mainstream Palestinian leadership signed the agreement, it apparently saw it as both the minimal and optimal program for the short term.[3] In any case, for the first time ever, the Palestinians came

3 As part of the implementation of the agreement, on December 14, 1998, the Palestinian National Council agreed, in the presence of the US president, to cancel articles of the Palestinian National Charter that deal with the destruction of Israel and appoint a committee for reformulating the charter. Owing to subsequent develop-

close to a state-situation: that is, the creation of a political entity
having independent central control within a given territory—itself
part of historical Palestine—and with the hope of expanding its
control and authority over these areas and their residents.

For the first time since 1948, the Palestinian leadership, or at least
part of it, returned to Palestine and settled among the people,
something that was not always comfortable either for the people or
the leadership. Many years of separate living under disparate conditions created differences in culture and in the interpretation of the
national interest, differences that were often exacerbated by generation gaps as well.

The PNA itself adopted state mannerisms and rituals. The PLO
chairman became the "President," those responsible for various port-
folios (the number of which grew to thirty-five by 2002) were termed
ministers, and the various departments became ministries. The PNA
adopted a flag and a national anthem, and sent diplomatic representatives abroad. The PNA established a radio station and several regional
television stations, which aired mostly government pronouncements
and sometimes even live broadcasts of the meetings of the Legislative
Council, whose own duties were mostly symbolic. The new government founded a judiciary system which attempted, without great
success, to be seen as independent of the executive authorities. A
short time after the signing of the Oslo Accords, on January 25,
1996, general elections were held in the PNA territories under

---

ments, this has still not been done, and today the legal status of the charter is not
clear. Two days earlier, on December 12, eight opposition groups from within the
PLO, Hamas, and Islamic Jihad met in Damascus to reaffirm their opposition to the
Oslo process and to the changes in the National Charter.

foreign supervision. The Palestinians saw the newly elected, eighty-eight seat Legislative Council as a parliament for all intents and purposes.

Fatah and the candidates identified with it received an overwhelming majority of the votes. To date, these are the only elections that have been held. One of the PNA's primary goals was the building of a shared national consciousness for all its residents and, if possible, for the Palestinians in exile too. Its primary tool for creating this common outlook was the establishment of an educational system with its own curriculum and textbooks, which would define the new Palestinian identity that was supposed to grow out of the revised sociopolitical entity represented by the PNA. Up until this time, the educational system had been mainly based on the Jordanian curriculum and emphasized preparing students for the Jordanian matriculation examinations (tawjihi). The rest of the curriculum was fleshed out by and taught in a system of United Nations Relief and Works Agencies' schools. An independent Palestinian curriculum—whose goals included teaching the national history and creating a national consciousness—had already begun to be formulated in the 1960s in Kuwait and Lebanon, yet the complete lack of autonomy made it impossible to carry out this task. The PNA tried to employ the best local educators and intellectuals to develop a curriculum and write textbooks, but this has proved to be a long and expensive process.

As a temporary substitute, attempts have been made to recruit the mass media for the task of building a Palestinian identity. Although there is no lack of enemies and adversaries to use in building the image of the "other" as opposed to the "us," there is still a need to avoid characterizing what is alien in an excessively vulgar fashion.

Thus, early on, the media confronted the dilemma over the need to broadcast positive propaganda for the peace process (before it fell apart to be replaced by armed confrontation) and to seek a reconciliation with Israel, and the need to present Zionism, Israel, and those who collaborated with it as an oppressive enemy. This balancing act became more difficult when the peace process was halted after the assassination of Rabin.

Prior to this, the struggle over the character of the future Palestinian state and society was reopened and became intertwined with the bitter struggle over the character of its relations with Israel and Judaism. The mainstream, which appeared to be the likely victors, struggled against a variety of opposition groups, mainly Islamic in character. The Islamic movement Hamas was internally divided between those who favored, at least during the initial euphoric stages of the peace process, integration with Arafat's popular new regime, and those who advocated adherence to the traditional goals of a holy war (jihad) against the Jews: the liberation of the Holy Land and, only then, the establishment of a theocratic Islamic state.

Considering its own best interests, the Islamic movement recognized that there were arguments both for and against renewing the jihad. Integration would force Fatah to take Hamas into consideration and grant them their proper place in the *sulta* (regime or government). That meant recognition, appropriate representation in national institutions, the conservation of the traditional values of Palestinian society, and, most significantly, a share of important positions and budget allocations. For those opposing the agreements, the renewal of guerilla warfare was intended to bring about the breakdown of agreements with Israel and prove that the PNA did not rule the

territories and could not provide Israel with what it most needed—
internal Israeli security. Between April 6, 1994 and August 21, 1996,
the Hamas and the Islamic Jihad movements succeeded in carrying
out a series of terrorist attacks in Israel's major cities by using suicide
bombers. Dozens of people were killed and hundreds wounded in the
middle of Israel's central cities. The concurrent operation of the
Israeli and Palestinian security forces, which was anchored in the
agreements between the two sides and was, from the standpoint of
the Israeli Government and public opinion, a necessary condition for
the continuation of the process, began to seem purposeless—because
the Palestinian authorities lacked either the ability or the willingness
to act against their brothers. It seemed as if the Islamic movement
had exercised a veto over the agreement that promised a reconciliation
between the Israelis and the Palestinians. Both leaderships had been
shamed in front of their respective constituencies and each other.

At that stage the response of the Israeli leadership as well as that
of public opinion was relatively moderate and restrained. Just two
years before, giving up territories within the Land of Israel to the
Palestinians, or the recognition of the PLO and talks with Arafat (who
was depicted for the Israeli public as a demon and the biggest enemy
of Israel and the Jews since the Nazi regime in Germany), were acts
as inconceivable from a Jewish-Israeli standpoint as was the idea of
giving up on Greater Palestine from a Palestinian standpoint. Nonetheless, the surprising and sudden agreement, which was led on the
one hand by the most highly admired, patriotic military leader in
Israel at the time, Yitzhak Rabin, and on the other by Yasser Arafat,
the very symbol of the Palestinian national struggle, was received by
both sides with a combination of relief, hope, questioning, uncer-

tainty, and rejection. The opposition in Israel had no alternative policy, and the hordes from both sides that would normally have opposed this "treason" did not yet take to the streets in protest (with the exception of the radical rightwing, religious-Zionist groups and some messianic Orthodox Jewish sects, especially Chabad).

Yet the massive harm done to Israeli citizens in the central areas of the big cities brought a change in the positive public opinion that had initially favored the series of agreements. It proved the opposition's claims that this was not peace. With each confirmation that terrorist acts were being renewed, Israel imposed closures of specific areas, enclosures of whole regions, and other collective punishments on the areas of the PNA as well as on areas that remained in Israeli control. Israel delayed carrying out further stages of the agreements (those which would have dealt with the transfer of additional areas to PNA control, the release of prisoners and captives, freedom of movement for students traveling between the West Bank and Gaza Strip, the transfer of tax funds to the PNA, and freedom of passage for Palestinian workers employed in Israel) and brought further talks to a halt. These and other delays increased the Palestinians' hatred of Israel and prompted more individuals and groups to join the renewed armed struggle. Following the increase in terrorist attacks in 2000, Israel decided to employ an as yet limited military force against all opponents and those who appeared to be responsible for the Palestinian guerilla fighting and to liquidate them methodically.

The vicious circle of terror and closures worsened the economic situation of the residents in the occupied territories (in the Gaza Strip there were reports of starvation) and increased the prestige of the Islamic resistance movement, leading to the evolution of new Palestinian heroes—the *shahadin*, or martyrs. The most well-known was Yehiyeh Iyaash, also known as the "engineer," who was most likely responsible for the preparation and direction of most suicide attacks occurring during this period. Eventually his murder by Israeli intelligence added to the heroic aura surrounding him.

In the beginning, the PNA did not have an intelligence service efficient enough to eliminate these activities, which threatened its authority and very existence. Also, Arafat did not want a direct, violent confrontation with these groups but preferred to divide and control them through co-option, bringing them under his control by granting posts and favors. It is very likely there was also a natural reluctance to hunt down and arrest individuals and groups who furthered the armed struggle and who were considered heroes and even saints by at least some of the Palestinian people. In addition, parts of the militia that the PNA had brought with them from abroad did not always manage to gain public trust and favor. These Palestinians, most of whom were born abroad, seemed like foreigners to the local society. When the PNA announced its intention to collect firearms, ammunition, and instruments of war from the local population, the Islamic movement objected outright. On November 22, 1994, bloody conflict between the Palestinian militia and the local residents broke out in Gaza, leading to the deaths of ten people.

One of the Palestinian hopes was that a change from Israeli control to PNA control would improve their standard of living, which had declined since the first Intifada and the expulsion of Palestinians from Kuwait—thereby halting the flow of money sent by workers there to relatives in the occupied territories. This hope had been based on the promise of an influx in outside capital and loans for the development of the economic infrastructure and social institutions. The entire peace process took place under the doubtful assumption that both sides had an economic interest in making peace work, and if these economic interests were nonexistent, then they should be created. Shimon Peres's vision of "a new Middle East" was also built on this assumption. Nevertheless, when it comes to such deep inter-ethnic and inter-religious conflicts, even if common economic interests are to be found, they never suffice in breaking down primordial feelings, especially in such a short time. It should also be mentioned that the Palestinians, like many other Arabs, feared the development of a sort of mercantile colonization, which would replace Israeli military rule in the region with technological and economic control.

By 1998 the influx of aid had indeed resulted in an economic improvement, but this improvement came to an abrupt end in September 2000 with the outbreak of the second Intifada and the subsequent deep recession which settled on the PNA's economy. In 2000, there was a 12 percent drop in the actual per capita income and another 19 percent drop in 2001. By the end of 2001, per capita income was 30 percent lower than in 1994, when the Gaza and Jericho Agreements had been signed. The World Bank estimated that half of the PNA's population was living below the poverty line. By September 2000, approximately seventy-five to eighty thousand Palestinians had lost their jobs in Israel and the settlements and another sixty thousand in the PNA territories itself

There is no doubt that while, at the beginning, autonomy raised hopes for an improved quality of life, these hopes went largely unrealized except, possibly, for the thin stratum of Palestinian society which benefited from the transfer of authority from Israeli military rule to the PNA. By and large, the opposite occurred. The standard of living for most Palestinians, especially those in the Gaza Strip, declined and a general decrease of 25 percent in the standard of living has been recorded since the beginning of the extended closures. The rumors of corruption that ran rampant and were often linked with the names of PNA leaders did not encourage development from below; instead they lent strength to the opposition, contributed to the demoralization of the population, and helped to raise the level of crime.

During the previous twenty years of occupation, Palestinian society distinguished itself by its expansion of non-governmental, volunteer associations and organizations. Many of these activists and service providers often received salaries and other compensation for their toils. At the beginning of the 1990s, these organizations employed between twenty and thirty thousand employees. Thus, in the absence of a state, the Palestinians had cultivated alternative mechanisms that had some characteristics of a civil society. Yet the budgets for these associations and institutions came largely from foreign sources. During the first Intifada, these organizations played an increasingly large role and, by the mid-90s, provided nearly half of all medical services, about a third of the educational services as well as counseling and support for former prisoners and the needy, and almost all aid and rehabilitation services for the disabled.

With the establishment of the PNA, it was only natural that it would take upon itself large portions of, if not all, the functions these associations had previously fulfilled. Indeed, within the framework of the PNA, different ministries were established for just this purpose. Yet it was difficult to build institutionalized civil services that would operate according to standards, and usually these offices became identified with the people who headed them—themselves close and loyal to the President. The PNA even began to assert its own authority over the voluntary organizations in an extreme fashion, either to demonstrate its own authority and power or because of the fear that, over time, parallel or subversive mechanisms would be established. Either way, it was understood that, at least in its initial stages, the nascent state was much less efficient and provided fewer services than did the voluntary organizations. It did not even solve the dilemma over whether veteran associations should be integrated into the state or confronted and wiped out.

15   From Near-Agreement to Stalemate

On November 4, 1995, Israeli Prime Minister Yitzhak Rabin was assassinated by a religious nationalist youth who hoped to stop the transfer of territories to PNA control. It was the culmination of months of unprecedented incitement and violent demonstrations against the Oslo Accords generally and Rabin personally, who was blamed for betraying the idea of the Greater Land of Israel. Tactics included the distribution of a poster showing Rabin in SS uniform. Opposition figures like Sharon and the new political star Benjamin Netanyahu played a major role in these incitements by using an unrestrained rhetoric of blood, land, and treason.[4] The fusion of the

4 On October 5, 1995, Sharon, Netanyahu, and Rafael Eitan attended a rally in Jerusalem and inflamed the participants so much that they called for the deaths of "Oslo criminals" Rabin and Peres. This incident has become part of the Israeli collective memory.

common interests between Islamic movements and their Israeli secularist rightwing and messianic fundamentalist counterparts was much stronger than the common interests of those supporting the problematic Oslo Accords.

As was previously mentioned, the Rabin administration was a minority government. Following Rabin's assassination, his partner Shimon Peres was unable to win the 1996 elections. One reason for his electoral defeat was the chain reaction following the assassination of Yayha Ayyash on January 6, 1996. Peres, who was acting Prime Minister at the time, authorized the "targeted killing" of Ayyash, a Hamas explosives and bomb-making expert and a hero to many in the Gaza Strip, in order to create for himself a tougher image before the election.[5] For several months prior to the assassination, Hamas had been quiescent and had not carried out any significant operations. This truce continued after Rabin's assassination. After the customary forty-day period of Muslim mourning, Hamas took its revenge in a series of bloody bombings inside Israel. The reaction of the Jewish-Israeli public was prompt. Both Labor's massive lead in the opinion polls and support for the reconciliation process melted away, while Likud and its rightwing hard line gained much support.

Peres and Labor also lost the support of Israeli Arabs. Many Israeli Arab (and some Jewish) voters of conscience decided to abstain from voting as a protest against Operation Grapes of Wrath, a series of air strikes against southern Lebanon in reprisal for the shelling by Hezbollah. These attacks caused about 200,000 inhabitants to flee

---

5 Indeed, contrary to previous practice in such cases, the Israeli Government admitted responsibility for the assassination and the Israeli media rejoiced over the successful liquidation.

their homes and the mistaken shelling of Kafr Qana caused the death of 100 Lebanese citizens.

At this point the settlers and rightwingers regained their political vitality. They invested all their efforts in electing Benjamin Netanyahu as Prime Minister. However, contrary to the expectations of many of his supporters, Netanyahu did not discard the "international agreements" (that is, Oslo), and even continued talks with the Palestinians under American sponsorship. He negotiated additional intermediary agreements, some of which were enacted, such as the return of Hebron (with the exception of the Jewish enclave), and the Wye River Memorandum (October 23, 1998). In the framework of the Wye agreement, control over additional Palestinian areas was transferred to the PNA, thus bringing the entire Palestinian urban population (with the exception of Jerusalem) and most of the refugee-camp population under PNA control. Portions of this agreement were carried out only later, during Barak's short term. Nevertheless, as a result of the Wye agreement, the radical right abandoned Likud, and established the National Union Party, which eventually brought about the fall of Netanyahu.

Even in the early stage of Netanyahu's administration, a change could be felt in the atmosphere and relations between Israel and the Palestinians. Mutual trust was beginning to founder. In addition to the new government's evident hostility toward the Palestinians, the opening of the Western Wall Tunnels further undermined the fragile agreements. These tunnels, which extended underneath the *Haram al-Sharif* (the Jewish Temple Mount), and were opened on September 25, 1996, were viewed by Muslims as a threat to the status of the holy places. Their opening incited demonstrations and riots during which about forty Palestinians were killed and 100 injured. Tensions also rose as construction plans were expanded into areas of Arab Jerusalem and in the settlements. A radical national rhetoric and scorn for Palestinians also increased feelings of alienation and served to further weaken the supervision of, and the restraint exercised over, Islamic elements (Hamas and Islamic Jihad), who renewed terrorist activities in Israeli cities. The increasing lack of personal security among the Jewish population in Israel also contributed to the fall of Netanyahu, and later that of Barak, although the personal conduct of both politicians and their inability to maintain decent personal relationships contributed as well.

On May 17, 1999, Ehud Barak was elected Prime Minister on the Labor Party ticket under a slogan promising the "continuation of the Rabin legacy." His election raised hopes for the restoration of trust between Israel and both the Palestinians in particular and the Arab World in general. Yet, at least during the beginning of his term, Barak seemed to be working under the traumatic cloud of Rabin's assassination. He tried to renew the diplomatic process through a coalition government composed of a "stable Jewish majority," that is, without the support of Israeli Arab voters, 95 percent of whom had cast their votes for him and to whom he owed a great deal of his success in Israel's first direct election for the premiership. Instead, from the beginning, the government cooperated with religious parties and those with rightwing tendencies (such as the National Religious Party, Shas, and the Russian Immigrant Party), and brought about the withdrawal from the coalition of the one Zionist party most dedicated to the reconciliation process, Meretz, simply to avoid even a resemblance to Rabin's coalition.

In retrospect, many, including Yossi Beilin for instance, suspected Barak of calculating his steps so that he could make his proposals look like huge compromises on Israel's part while knowing that they would be completely unacceptable to the Palestinians. Thus he could seemingly unmask the true face of the Palestinians and declare "Israel has no real partner in peace." It seems more likely that Barak genuinely believed that Israel was strong enough to coerce the Palestinians into accepting an agreement based on his own conditions.[6] That is why he spent his first year in office attempting to reach an agreement with Syria in order to isolate the Palestinians. In Barak's own words, "achieving peace with Syria would greatly limit the Palestinians' ability to widen the conflict." But the xenophobic Hafez Assad was not in the proper mood to make peace with the Israelis—even in exchange for the entire territory occupied in 1967 and re-occupied in 1973—because in doing so he would be forced to open his borders to strangers and to new and dangerous ideas.

And indeed Barak's approach was different from Rabin's:[7] he refused to continue implementing the agreement in stages that would eventually lead to a complete withdrawal to the 1967 borders in

6 Another reason why Beilin's assertion doesn't make sense is that even an inexperienced politician like Barak would not sacrifice his political career just to prove that the Palestinians would not be able to accept the most generous (from the Israeli point of view) offer ever made to them or the most far-reaching one possible.

7 As the Chief of Staff during Rabin's premiership, he objected to the Oslo agreement, a fact that he did not explain or even mention during his electoral campaign and that was ignored by the mass media that supported him, almost completely, against Netanyahu. Public opinion in Israel seems to ignore events from all but the most recent past and accountability is almost completely nonexistent in Israeli political culture, a fact that is exemplified by the election and re-election of Ariel Sharon.

accordance with the accepted interpretation of Resolution 242 of the UN Security Council, November 22, 1967. Instead, he thought that with a government coalition of various rightwing and centrist parties he could negotiate a final agreement with the Palestinians that would include the establishment of a demilitarized Palestinian state and acceptance on their part of "an end to the conflict" without the need to return to the 1967 borders. At the same time, he hoped to reduce the refugee problem to one that could be addressed with a mere admission of moral responsibility for creating it, to keep the Temple Mount under sole Jewish control, and to avoid vacating the large blocks of Jewish settlements near the Green Line. Barak thought he could bypass his own government and even the Knesset by appealing directly to the people through a referendum—an unprecedented act in Israeli political culture—for approval of the agreement he was certain he could reach with the Palestinian leadership.

However, his initial (and it later became apparent, only) success was the withdrawal of Israeli armed forces from southern Lebanon, where a desperate guerilla war had been waged by Hezbollah, a group created as a response to Israel's 1982 invasion, against the occupying Israeli army.

It seemed that Barak had no idea whatsoever what kind of final agreement would be acceptable to the Palestinians, and probably had no idea what kind of agreement he wanted except that it would include gaining maximal concessions from the Palestinians while paying a minimal political and territorial price. He also lacked both substantial political experience and a knowledgeable political staff, and ran the prime minister's office like a military general staff. It was, furthermore, not at all clear that the Palestinian (or Israeli) leadership and public were politically prepared to make the concessions necessary to "end the conflict" after the initial euphoria over the Oslo Accords had worn off.

16 The Camp David Debacle[8]

From July 11 to 25, 2000, the American President Bill Clinton, in cooperation with Ehud Barak, held an Israeli–Palestinian peace summit at Camp David, a place loaded with symbolism because the Israeli–Egyptian peace accord was negotiated there in 1979. The summit failed, with tragic consequences for both sides. The Americans and Israelis blame the Palestinians generally and Yasser Arafat personally for the debacle, while the Palestinians put the blame on the American and Israeli teams, although each side retrospectively took some responsibility for mismanagement on the tactical level. To blame one or the other side has become part of the conflict, and is not the aim of the present chapter. However, this issue is important in understanding the causes and dynamics that led to the collapse and fragmentation of the Israeli peace camp and Ariel Sharon's unexpected political comeback.

Yasser Arafat had reservations about the summit from the beginning. He did not trust Barak, for good reason. Barak failed to implement additional stages of the interim agreements (even those Netanyahu had agreed to); he refused to freeze settlements, and during his short term, their number increased by more then 10 percent; he did not

8 In referring to the Camp David talks here, I include the entire series of negotiations between the Israelis and the Palestinians during this period, including those in May 2000 (in Stockholm), July 2000 (at Camp David), and February 2001, mainly in the US and Egypt (in Taba).

release prisoners and camp detainees and, as mentioned above, he made overtures to Syria in an effort to isolate the Palestinians. Furthermore, Arafat did not believe that an American president could serve as an honest and impartial broker between the Israelis and Palestinians. Moreover, he was convinced that a successful summit must be better prepared and that the Barak–Clinton summit was premature in the light of the unofficial Israeli proposals made during the May 2000 meeting in Stockholm. Arafat's initial feelings may or may not have been a self-fulfilling prophecy, but whatever the case, Clinton's patronizing tone and Barak's notorious arrogance did not create a leisurely atmosphere conducive to fertile and creative negotiations among equal parties. Barak's suggestions toward the end of the talks, and Clinton's bridging proposals, were not far from being acceptable to the Palestinian team and could have been used as a basis for further negotiations, but it seems they were rejected by Arafat probably because of the flawed dynamics that developed before and during the talks.[9] Shlomo Ben Ami, Barak's chief negotiator, described Barak's starting position:

> Barak showed me a map that included the Jordan Rift Valley and was a kind of very beefed-up Allon Plan. He was proud of the fact that

9 For the map of Israeli proposals in Camp David compared with the proposals submitted during the Taba talks, see the website of *Le Monde Diplomatique*: http:// www.monde-diplomatique.fr/cartes/taba2001. It is interesting to notice that there is a surprising similarity in the descriptions of the internal dynamics of the talks, even among those who disagree about who is ultimately responsible for their failure. I am referring to, among others, Robert Malley, Clinton's Special Assistant for Arab–Israeli Affairs from 1998 to 2001, who tends to put the major responsibility for the failure on the Israeli and American teams, Dennis Ross, Clinton's special envoy to the Middle East, who supports unequivocally the Clinton–Barak version, Shlomo Ben Ami, one of the chief Israeli negotiators, and Ehud Barak himself.

his map would leave Israel with about a third of the territory. If I remember correctly, he gave the Palestinians only 66 percent of the land. Ehud [Barak] was convinced that the map was extremely logical. He had a kind of patronizing, wishful-thinking, naive approach, telling me enthusiastically, "Look, this is a [Palestinian] state; to all intents and purposes it looks like a state."

Several other factors, in addition to those already mentioned, combined to cause the fatal failure. First of all, neither participant in the negotiations possessed a clear and well-defined vision of his own goals. The immediate aim of the Palestinians, who were aware of their own weakness, was to minimize their damages. This led them toward a calculated passivity that caused them both to fail to make their own proposals and to reject any proposal made by the Israelis or the Americans, who were suspected, no doubt correctly, of coordinating their offers with Israel. During the initial stages, this may have been a highly rational tactic because it forced the Israelis to improve their subsequent proposals, but when the rejection became automatic, even as the Israelis made more realistic suggestions, it became disastrous. At least once, though, Arafat abandoned his calculated passivity and made an informal proposal to Clinton. To quote Ben Ami:

Yesterday [July 17], Arafat made a proposal to Clinton in relation to the scenario of the previous night.[10] "He [Arafat] is ready to concede

---

10 At one stage Ben Ami—during a simulation game with some of the Palestinian team's members—wrongly concluded that there had been a breakthrough in the

between 8 and 10 percent of the territory. He told Clinton: "I leave the matter of the [territorial] swap in your hands, you decide." He is ready for security arrangements as they will be decided. He places the emphasis on an international force. We will find a solution on the refugee issue, too. Everything now stands or falls over Jerusalem. Arafat wants a solution there that he can live with. . . ." But some time later Arafat retracted [his offer]. He conveyed a note to Clinton in which he retracted.

In reaction to the Palestinians' obstinacy, Barak adopted a tactic more appropriate to negotiations in a bazaar. He began with the costliest offer to the Palestinians (close to the Allon Plan) but hinted that it was just an opening position. The partners in this negotiation, including, probably, Barak himself, did not know the end point of this bargaining process. Additionally, because he needed to keep the views of his constituency in mind, each of Barak's proposals was a "non-proposal" or "non-paper" (an experimental balloon in diplomatic terminology), so that he could preserve his standing with his hawkish and religious Cabinet. Moreover, until the last stages of the negotiations, in December and January, his team never forwarded a complete package of proposed settlements for all the major unresolved issues. Each issue—like the exchange of territories, borders, settlement blocs, refugees, airspace, and water rights, etc.—was dealt with separately by different negotiators, a tactic that does not allow for trade-offs or the possibility of quid pro quos. Each party also was

---

negotiations on the issue of the status of the so-called Holy Basin, which includes all the holy shrines of the three religions in Jerusalem.

talking and thinking in its own meta-historical and mythical narratives and codes. An excellent example of this was the angry dispute over whether the ruins of the biblical Temple of King Solomon were or were not lying under the Second Temple. Arafat argued that there is nothing under the *Haram al-Sharif*, and if a First Temple existed, it was in Nablus. This meta-historical argument deeply offended the secular Jewish negotiators, who promptly concluded that Arafat rejected the historical ties of the Jewish people to Jerusalem and the whole land. The Christian Protestant Bill Clinton was also hurt; and he told Arafat "not only the Jews but I, too, believe that the remains of Solomon's temple lie under its surface. That is what my minister told me in church last Sunday." At this point, one of Clinton's Jewish aides attracted the President's attention and said that he should tell Arafat that this was his personal opinion, not an official American position. Thus, for both sides, the sovereignty over the so-called sacred basin (the area outside the Old City wall that includes the City of David and the Tombs of the Prophets on the road to the Mount of Olives) became a major issue that seemed to be less negotiable than the right of return for refugees or the evacuation of the settlements.

The final blow to the peace process, and one strongly connected to the mythological dimension of the conflict, was the spectacular and highly publicized visit by Ariel Sharon to the Temple Mount, which is, of course, near al-Aqsa, the third holiest shrine in Islam. The visit triggered a new, violent Palestinian outburst of popular protest and a violent Israeli response. The conflict soon escalated into an inter-communal war. The remaining negotiations were conducted in the shadow of this new cycle of violence, which was soon given the emotionally and religiously loaded name—the al-Aqsa Intifada. The

Israelis were sure that the violence was pre-planned in order to extort more concessions, and the Palestinian leadership perceived it as a popular warning against any agreement that smacked of surrender.

Under these circumstances, the Palestinian–Israeli talks had no chance of producing an agreement, especially since the Oslo Accords were constructed according to Kissinger's doctrine of "constructive ambiguity," a concept that is inherently unworkable in this type of conflict. The idea behind constructive ambiguity is to get the negotiating parties to agree to some very general principles and let each party interpret them according to its own wishful thinking. It may have been a brilliant idea for achieving agreements between the United States and China or Vietnam, nations separated by thousands of miles, but not for two ethnically diverse populations living in such intimate proximity to one another. In such a situation, any small friction or incident can cause immense tension and has the potential to become an uncontrollable conflagration.

Thus, the Palestinians' understanding of the Oslo Accords—the base line for the final-status agreement—was that giving up 78 percent of the original territory of historical Palestine and recognizing the Jewish state's right to exist in the region were far-reaching and painful concessions that were inadequately repaid. A significant portion of the Palestinian population regarded Arafat's signing of the Accords as national treason. In fact, the pragmatic Fatah leadership had imagined an agreement identical to the Israeli–Egyptian formula: peace and recognition in exchange for *all* of the territory captured during the war of 1967. The Palestinians took Netanyahu's 1996 election as a sign that a majority of Israeli Jews rejected the principles and the spirit of Oslo, without taking into account the fact that the Israeli

public's rejection of the Accords and the delay in the implementation of their different clauses were in a measure caused by the
violence generated by Palestinian (mainly Islamic) opposition to the
Accords.

The election of Barak provided renewed hopes, but these gradually
evaporated. Even when the PNA controlled most of the population of
the Palestinian cities, refugee camps, and villages, the roads between
them were mostly under Israeli control. Israeli outposts, checkpoints,
armed settlers, and closures still restricted the Palestinian people's
freedom and caused them daily humiliations six years after Oslo. The
Islamic movement provided them with an alternative worldview, self-
esteem, and hope. The al-Aqsa Intifada was, and still is, a rebellion
not only against Israeli oppression and occupation but also against
their own leadership and regime (sulta)—which is regarded as too
submissive to Israel and domestically corrupt. Additionally—and this
is true on the other side of the barricade as well—the mixture of
fanatic nationalism and religious fundamentalism has a strong appeal,
especially during times of crisis.

The first Intifada was a genuine popular and civil uprising; the
second quickly developed into an armed revolt. Unlike the previous
Intifada, there was no longer an Israeli military presence in the
Palestinian camps and towns; thus, the violence was directed against
settlers on the roads and toward the civilian population within Israel.
Very soon, members of the Palestinian militias joined in, either
individually or in groups, using firearms against Israelis and escalating
the violence, which turned into ethnic warfare between the Israelis
and the PNA by early 2002. The Israelis tried to activate the
Palestinian Preventive Security Forces and the common security

committees—mostly without success—against the attackers and also retaliated without cooperating with the Palestinian leadership.

The most frightening weapon used by the so-called military wings of two Islamic movements, Hamas and the Islamic Jihad, was the suicide bomber. Suicide bombing was first introduced by the Islamic resistance movement, which copied the tactic from Islamists in Indonesia opposing British rule. Subsequently, other groups, including some Fatah units, adopted it following its success.

Initially, suicide bombing was a response to the enormous asymmetry of power between the Israeli military and Palestinian fighters. Being precisely guided human missiles, suicide bombers caused heavy, mainly civilian, casualties among the Israelis, paralyzed daily life almost completely, and badly damaged Israeli morale. The suicide bombers and their families won great honor among the Palestinians as supreme martyrs for their patriotic cause. Before and during the talks, Arafat and the entire leadership of the PNA faced a major dilemma in responding ideologically and morally to the Islamists and particularly to the phenomenon of the suicide bombers. An open clash with the Islamists meant a civil war, but the continuation of their jihad gave the Israelis an important card to play in refusing to implement agreements. After Sharon was elected Prime Minister, it gave him a powerful argument to use in urging the United States to include Arafat and the whole PNA in their fight against "world terror" following September 11. Therefore, Arafat tried to either co-opt the Islamists or reach agreements with them to suspend the terrorist attacks that were causing irreversible damage to the national movement. However, he eventually failed because his inability to handle the Israelis as the Palestinians desired had damaged his prestige and authority. Additionally, his own men (especially the so-called Al-Aqsa Brigades), in competition with the rival groups, initiated terror attacks, including suicide bombings. Thus, Arafat found himself in a trap: he could not stop the terror because he was weak and indecisive, yet the continuing attacks made him even weaker because they hampered his ability to manage proper negotiations at Camp David and Taba.

Eventually, the Israelis found a way not only to handle the suicide bombings, but to exploit it for their own purposes, as will be demonstrated later. The horror caused by the suicide bombings was used to gain domestic and international legitimacy for the unrestrained use of Israeli military power and later to dismantle gradually the PNA and void the Oslo Accords.

The suicide bombers in particular and the increasing chain of violence in general were not by any means the reason for the failure of the negotiations at Camp David and Taba, but they added considerably to the difficulties faced by both parties.[11] The immediate result of the Camp David debacle and the escalation in Palestinian terrorism was the evaporation of what little still remained of Jewish and Arab popular support for reconciliation and compromise with the other party. This wave of disappointment and anger paved the road

11 Actually the suicide bombings preceded the talks and began almost immediately after the Declaration of Principles was made public. Since then, according to the Israeli security service account that was published in the media at the end of 2002, 206 suicide bombers have been sent on these desperate missions in the last decade. Some of the explosions have been prevented. During the first two years of the al-Aqsa Intifada, the Palestinians sent out 145 suicide bombers, 40 of whom were identified as being affiliated with Fatah, 52 were Hamas men, and 35 belonged to Islamic Jihad; the rest could not be connected with any particular group.

for Ariel Sharon's comeback and the perception of his victory as a mandate for the "patriotic mission" of nullifying the agreement with the Palestinians, gradually destroying the Palestinian National Authority, committing politicide against the Palestinians, and regaining control over the Land of Israel in its entirety. This was an unprecedented victory for the self-appointed national camp in Israel and has intensified the current chaotic situation in the region today.

PART III

THE COMEBACK

17 The Diversification of Israeli Society

The ascendancy of Ariel Sharon's political philosophy—or the socio-political culture and reality that allowed him to be re-elected in January 2003 without any significant opposition, accountability, or checks and balances—is no accident. Sharon's ideology entered a power-vacuum left behind by the established Ashkenazi political elite. This elite was never homogenous and their core beliefs were contradictory in important respects. However, it was precisely these contradictions that contributed to the almost unprecedented success of the Zionist enterprise and to understand them it is useful to examine the original version of Israel's national identity.

This collective identity includes two basic orientations which both complement and conflict with one another and are, in fact, almost mutually exclusive: the one is a primordial or tribal identity, a mixture of religious and nationalistic orientations; the other is a civil identity based on concepts of universal human and civil rights. The relative weight and salience of these identities, which shape the rules governing the behavior of the Israeli state, were always the focus of a continuing struggle among the various segments of the state and society.

Participation in the primordial polity depends on ethnic and religious identity. The boundary of legitimate society encompasses all Jews (including those in the Diaspora), but excludes all non-Jews as equal members in the state. The ideal legislature is based on the traditional Jewish religious codex, the *Halacha*; and, at least as a utopian desire, the aim is to transform the current polity into a system ruled by Jewish law. The world is perceived as a binary order of "us" (the Jews) versus "them" (the rest of the world), the latter being a homogenous and hostile entity. An eternal and inevitable struggle for survival is a basic characteristic of the cosmic order. There are no substantial differences between all the historical enemies of the Jewish people, such as the Assyrians, Romans, Christians, Nazis, and Arabs. All are inscribed in the Jewish collective memory as having genocidal intentions. While war should be postponed, it is nevertheless inevitable. In this view, Jewish survival is also threatened by an inherent urge toward self-destruction that leads Jews to abandon Jewish culture and embrace hedonistic gentile cultures like Hellenism, Christianity, the Enlightenment, and modernism, thus threatening the Jewish people with moral decay and cultural erosion. Thus the battle for survival involves wielding the sword against both the enemies outside and the traitors within. Any criticism of Jews, the Jewish state, or its policies, is considered anti-Semitic, while Jewish traitors are to be vigorously denounced. The more primordial segments of society, especially those fringe groups located on the end of the continuum, unequivocally prefer Jewishness over democracy as the guiding light of the polity. More sophisticated elite groups talk about "Jewish democracy," a system in which only Jews are entitled to collective or national civil rights, while non-Jewish minorities at best enjoy individual rights, if necessary.

However, a pure and exclusive Jewish state, whatever it means, is considered highly preferable. Democracy is explicitly not a Jewish value and if it is used for the purposes of internal or external public relations, what is actually meant is a *Herrenvolk* democracy.[1]

The second part of the Israeli collective identity, the civil one, is essentially a mirror image of the first. Membership within the sociopolitical boundaries of the state is based on the notion of citizenship. Here universal duties (such as the payment of taxes, military service, and obedience to the law) are balanced by universal rights (welfare, services, social security, justice, law and order, civil liberties and freedoms). Laws are adopted according to secular universalistic principles by a democratically elected parliament, which follows the standards of the Western Enlightenment as shaped by the French and American Revolutions. Society is perceived as a pluralistic entity, legitimately divided among subcultures that are empowered to act within a common public sphere, sometimes called civil society. Overt and covert conflicts are an integral part of the social order, but

1 In the current political culture, a state must claim that it is democratic, in part because an undemocratic state exposes itself to attack by rival states seeking to democratize it, something that happened to Afghanistan and Iraq. In this context, it is important to note that on June 24, 2002 President George W. Bush stated that the establishment of a Palestinian state in the unspecified future was conditional on an end to terror and a change in the present Palestinian leadership (by free election), and the democratization of the PNA.

are controlled, managed, and even resolved by sociopolitical mechanisms such as courts, the state bureaucracy, and agents of civil society
(e.g., NGOs, political parties, mass media). At the center of society
stands the individual, replete with rights and interests. International
relations are based on webs of crosscutting interests, and the state as
an actor in the international arena plays in accordance with its
changing interests, maneuvering between allies, rivals, and enemies.
War is considered avoidable through a wise mix of military might
(deterrence) and diplomacy. Actually, the civil orientation separated
the Israeli state conceptually and psychologically from its geographical
and cultural milieu and led to its being perceived by others in the
Middle East as a kind of historical accident.[2] The tribal aspect of the
Israeli identity does locate Israel in the Middle East, but sees the
country as being in eternal conflict—culturally, politically, and militarily—with its environment.

Although the original ruling classes of this immigrant-settler society
possessed both the tribal and universal parts of the Israeli collective
identity, they knew how to balance them successfully and how to shape
government policies to fit both sets of principles, at least in regard to
the Jewish bubble of the society. However, great waves of immigration
brought far-reaching demographic shifts that were followed by political
and cultural changes. During the first three decades of Israel's existence, the established Ashkenazi political elites[3]—many of whom

2 Since the early 1950s, the dream of Ben-Gurion and many others had been the
acceptance of Israel into the nascent European Union as a full member. Most of
Israel's international, cultural, and athletic events occur in Europe.

3 Socially, if not culturally, they are similar to the North American WASP
population.

appeared in the first part of this book—were able to maintain the old order by subjugating the new immigrants, especially those from Islamic countries, culturally and politically.[4] When this hegemonic class began its steady decline, a more tribal and ethnocentric definition of the collective identity arose. These minority groups did not yet have enough political power and skill to form their own dominant organizations so they turned to the veteran rightwing chauvinistic opposition, the Herut Party (later they turned to Likud) under Menachem Begin to express their hatred of their "socialist" oppressors and the secular "non-Jewish" culture they were forced to adopt. Thus, the 1977 election was not only the result of public dissatisfaction after the 1973 War, but was also the result of a coalition of underprivileged Jewish groups responding to populist chauvinistic slogans like "doing good for the people" and rallying around the paternalistic figure of Menachem Begin. Two additional political processes reinforced the creation of a stable and growing coalition of various embittered groups, not all of whom had good cause to feel aggrieved. The first process was the creation and growth of Shas, a sociopolitical movement of second-generation Oriental and religiously oriented Jews. Originally, the Shas leadership, and particularly its founding father Rabbi Ovadia Yosef, held comparatively moderate attitudes toward the Jewish–Arab conflict. Nevertheless, its constituency has increasingly pushed it toward a more hard-line position and it is now an integral part of the political right.

4 Many of the new immigrants were settled in peripheral frontier locations, including the 450 Arab villages and neighborhoods vacated in 1948. They were also rehabilitated, a process that meant many people who had been middle-class merchants or artisans in their countries of origin were now forced to become peasants. Their culture was regarded as primitive and they were defined as second-class Jews. At the same time, they were secularized by force.

A second immigrant group, in many ways a mirror image of the Jews from Islamic countries, is the Russian-speaking immigrants who currently number more than one million people. At first, they were the political hope of the Ashkenazi elite. Most of them were middle-class professionals with profiles similar to those of the ruling elite. However, they preferred to be absorbed into the middle class while retaining a distinct cultural identity—something their large numbers allowed them to do. Even though most of them are strongly secular and anti-clerical, they possess a strong nationalistic orientation that they brought with them from their country of origin.[5] In the Soviet lands, they were a persecuted minority. Now being a part of the majority in their new homeland, their interpretation of patriotism is the persecution and oppression of minorities. Coming from a geographically large country, they perceived Israel's minuscule territory as a major handicap and couldn't see how a healthy nation could give up any part of its territory. The Russians viewed Israel's readiness to make territorial concessions to the Palestinians as a sign of weakness, even as treason, and their political behavior is intended to heal the nation of its weaknesses and maladies.

An additional sociopolitical change occurring during the last two decades has been the increasing political activity by many anti-Zionist

5 About 30 percent of them are not Jews according to strict Halachic criteria ("a person is considered a Jew if born to a Jewish mother—but not a Jewish father—or was converted. The conversion must be in accordance with the Orthodox interpretation of the Halacha)." Moreover, about 10–15 percent of these new immigrants are professed Christians. They are forming a new category in Israeli society and are considered Jews (not just Israelis) by nationality and Christians by religion. The political scientist Ian Lustick argues that the demographic problem (exposed in chapter 2) is transforming Israel from a Jewish state to a non-Arab state.

Orthodox Jewish groups who joined the rightwing parliamentary bloc. This was made possible by the activities of the young guard of the religious Zionists who, in the mid-1970s, attained a central role in Israeli political life through their role as the vanguard of the settlement movement, especially in the West Bank, which was regarded as the heart of the ancient biblical kingdom. The activities of the religious Zionists blurred the boundaries between religion and nationalism, thus making it easier for the anti-Zionist parties to participate in political life.

These correlations between social origins and membership in the rightwing political bloc are major generalizations, but they are statistically correct, especially in periods of crisis and political polarization, like the one following the failure of the Camp David negotiations. However, many Jews originating in Russia or Islamic countries vote for leftist parties, and others are considered floating voters who frequently switch their votes back and forth between right and left blocs.

The recent decline of the leftist parliamentary bloc was also caused by the withdrawal of Israeli Arab citizens from the electoral process following the events of October 2000. In that month, residents of almost all the Arab towns and villages took to the streets in angry protest, blocking roads, throwing stones, and shouting slogans denouncing the state and its policies. In some mixed towns (Nazareth, Acre, and even Haifa, a city well known for its comfortable inter-ethnic relations) clashes broke out between Jewish and Arab residents. The police reacted with the unbridled violence often used by occupying forces in the West Bank and Gaza, including the use of live ammunition. This time, however, the shooting was directed at citizens of the state. Thirteen Arabs and one Jew were killed, about 700 were wounded, and hundreds more arrested. The Arab citizens of Israel felt they were losing the political strength they had gradually built in the two previous decades. They also felt betrayed by most of the Jewish partners with whom they had tried to bring about a historic reconciliation between Jews and Arabs by working together for the establishment of a Palestinian state alongside Israel.

All these political and demographic changes swung the pendulum of Israeli nationalism—which is always in motion between its civic and primordial extremes—to the extreme tribal end of its arc. This is the background of the political and military developments described in the third part of this volume.

18   The New Sharon

Following Sharon's first election, in which the electorate voted directly for the Prime Minister, some analysts in Israel and abroad expected a reborn Ariel Sharon, an Israeli version of de Klerk or de Gaulle who would free Israel from its colonies and evacuate the Israeli *pied noirs*.[6] After all, Sharon was raised in the bosom of the pragmatic

6 At first, the Israeli electoral system was country-wide and required voters to vote for a list of politicians or a party. The head of the party that won the most seats in the Knesset was invited by the President to form a government coalition, a necessary step because in the entire history of the country, no one party has ever succeeded in gaining an absolute majority of the 120 Knesset seats. This system seems to encourage the fragmentation of the Knesset into many small parties and increases the ability of these parties to extort concessions. To avoid this, a grass-roots movement at the end of 1990s forced the parliament to adopt a dual system of

Labor Party and was the man who evacuated the Jewish settlements in the Sinai. And indeed, in some measure, the Sharon of 2001–3 is not the Sharon of 1982. He realized that he had to create both domestic and international support for his policies and that it is impossible to achieve long-term goals with naked power alone. Today, his rhetoric is relatively moderate and ambiguous—in contrast with his deeds on the ground. He declared several times that, after the Palestinians had the level of their aspirations reduced, a peace could be achieved and that this would demand painful concessions from Israel. He also said that some autonomous Palestinian state should be established within five years or so and refused to rescind this declaration, even in the face of pressure from extreme rightwing politicians, including Benjamin Netanyahu, who challenged him in a primary held shortly before the 2003 general election. At the same time, he vowed that under no circumstances would he uproot any Jewish settlement. However, Sharon never revealed the slightest detail of any plan—even though it is well known he is a daring and highly sophisticated tactician. There are also no signs that he has changed any of his basic perceptions of the Israeli–Palestinian conflict.

In an in-depth interview published last year in *Ha'aretz Magazine*,

---

elections, one a direct election for the prime minister's office, and another election for the different political parties. Netanyahu and, in his previous election, Sharon, were brought into power by the system of personal election. However, this new system weakened the major parties even more, allowing voters to vote for small parties representing their particular interests and then for the premiership to express their general preference for the right or left blocs. For these reasons, the old system was re-established and Sharon's second election was the result of his being the head of Likud, the party winning the greatest number of seats in the general election.

Sharon made it clear that his historic mission is to complete the job that was not finished in the 1948 War:

> The War of Independence has not ended. No, 1948 was just one chapter. If you ask me whether the State of Israel is capable of defending itself today, I say yes, absolutely. And if you ask me whether the State of Israel is facing the danger of war, I say no. But are we living here securely? No. And therefore it is impossible to say that we have completed the work and that now we can rest on our laurels.

The journalist did not ask him what exactly he meant by writing "another chapter" in the War of Independence and, in this unique document, he left his intentions open to many possible interpretations, even as he left no doubt about his own meta-historical perception of his role.

Perhaps his wisest political move was made promptly after his first election to the premiership, when he offered the Labor Party an opportunity to join a so-called National Unity Government, despite the fact that he did not need them to establish a coalition and could have formed a stable and purely rightwing government. In fact, this was a well-calculated move directed primarily at Shimon Peres and Benjamin Ben Eliezer. Ben Eliezer (nicknamed "Fuad")—who immigrated as a child from Iraq to Israel in 1950—was the first non-Ashkenazi chairman of the Labor Party and a symbol of the party's efforts to accommodate itself to changing social realities. Ben Eliezer spent most of his adult life (about thirty years) in the military, and was for a certain time under Sharon's command. He was known as a docile admirer of his superiors (even during the Lebanese War), was considered a hawk, and filled some peripheral posts in Barak's Cabinet. Sharon's invitation to serve as Minister of Defense was an offer he could not refuse, as he hoped to strengthen his weak political profile. Peres was another story. An aging politician, he is, despite his international respectability, considered an eternal loser in Israel (last time he lost the party's chairmanship to Ben Eliezer) and a wishy-washy, cynical politician. Peres can adapt his attitude to any political circumstance, becoming alternately hawkish or dovish, a supporter of a Palestinian state or an opponent of it. Predictably, Ben Eliezer and Peres accepted Sharon's offer and explained their decision to join his Cabinet by the need to restrain Sharon, to counterbalance the extreme right, and to ensure the continuation of the Oslo process.[7]

Despite strong objections from some prominent Labor Party figures, Ben Eliezer and Peres coerced the defeated party to join the National Unity Government.[8] Soon it became quite clear that even if the Labor ministers wanted to influence Sharon's Cabinet or to

7 Benjamin Netanyahu fell into a similar trap when he accepted Sharon's suggestion that he join his Cabinet as Foreign Minister following Labor's departure from the National Unity Government. Netanyahu's reason for accepting the offer was probably his belief that he would be in a better position to attack Sharon for his overly soft policy toward the Palestinians if he had a ministerial position, but as a cabinet member his attacks lacked credibility.

8 Among the main objectors were the dovish Yossi Beilin, Abraham Burgh, and Haim Ramon, who criticized Ben Eliezer for selling out the party's ideology to advance his own political career, a prediction completely fulfilled during the 2003 election. Another hawkish Labor politician who joined Sharon's government was the former "civilian" governor of the West Bank, Ephraim Sneh. Sharon even succeeded in recruiting Ms. Dahlia Rabin-Philosoff, Yitzhak Rabin's daughter, as vice Minister of Defense.

oppose him from within—and it was doubtful that they wanted to—they had no chance of doing so. The National Unity Government eventually collapsed on October 30, 2002, when Labor voted against the budget on the pretext that it allocated too much money to the occupied territories at the expense of welfare and the development of Israeli towns. In fact, the move was taken after several national surveys showed that continuing its participation in the coalition would cause Labor to vanish from the Israeli political map. But seemingly it was too late both for the party and the country—as the January 2003 election results proved.[9]

Sharon's gains from Labor's participation in his first government were obvious: he managed to crush internal political opposition by forming the largest government in Israel's history and to gain an unprecedented domestic legitimacy.[10] The man who many consider a war criminal by any standard, and who had been Israel's most notorious politician for twenty years, had become the country's most popular and highly regarded premier.

It is true that most of Sharon's constituency—young people and new immigrants—have never heard about his deeds and regard the 1982 debacle as simply so much history, yet even those who happen

9 Amram Mitzna, the badly defeated Labor leader, preferred to try to rebuild his party's credibility and electorate from within opposition. Sharon replaced Labor with the "centrist" (in fact secular-chauvinist) party, Shinui, that did very well in the election, based on a selfish middle-class electorate, and headed by an Israeli version of Le Pen, the journalist Yossef (Tommy) Lapid.

10 The only two medium-sized Jewish parties that remained outside of the coalition were the leftist Meretz and the centrist Shinui. Later some extreme rightwing factions left the Cabinet to protest against Sharon's soft policy toward the Palestinians but continued to support the government from outside against the left.

to know about his past actions do not regard them as sins. On the contrary, Sharon is considered a hero, a savior who prevented Egypt from annihilating the state, "the King of Israel." It is symptomatic of Israel's current political climate that the media did not publish the candidate's biography before the 2001 elections, that Sharon's fairly honest autobiography was never published in Hebrew, and that Uzi Benziman's biography was relatively flattering and focused mainly on Sharon's personal characteristics.

Thus, the only Zionist opposition party is Meretz, which is ruled by Yossi Sarid with an iron fist. Sarid does indeed exhibit the traditional rhetoric and positions of the peace camp, but lacks the courage needed to become an assertive opposition leader. Unlike the original founder and leader of the party, the lawyer and civil-rights activist Shulamit Alloni, Sarid was a cautious politician, deeply concerned about remaining within the Zionist consensus (whose imaginary boundaries are drawn by Sarid himself), an approach that led the party to a major defeat in the 2003 election and the abdication of Sarid from his chairperson position. This approach has limited the party's effectiveness precisely at the time when it might be able to become a genuine alternative to both Likud and Labor—the latter, despite going into opposition, is still not viewed as an ideological alternative to the former.

In fact, what prevented Meretz from becoming a real opposition party with the potential to alter the self-destructive course of the Israeli state was its unwillingness to take the politically risky but necessary steps to end the present conceptual impasse. Contrary to what other representatives of Meretz, like Naomi Chazan or their elder stateswoman Shulamit Alloni, have claimed, there were two major issues that Sarid backed away from: war crimes and conscientious objectors. Sarid and other veteran and so-called liberal leaders of the party, like Amnon Rubinstein, perceived opposition to war crimes and support for conscientious objectors to be outside the Zionist consensus and therefore beyond the pale of permissible debate.

19   The Third Attempt At Politicide

Although no one knows Sharon's intentions, his acts—and in some matters, his failure to act—are straightforward and do not leave much room for interpretation. During the first night of Passover, on March 27, 2002, a suicide bomber killed twenty-nine people and wounded 150 others who were attending a Seder, the ritual Passover meal, at a small hotel in the coastal town of Netanya. Two days later, Israel called up many of its reserve units and declared the beginning of Operation Defensive Shield. The operation had been planned long before, but the suicide attack, which had stirred up domestic and world public opinion, provided the perfect pretext for beginning the process of politicide against the Palestinian people.

Attempts to commit politicide against the Palestinians are not new and have recurred frequently—first with the cooperation of Transjordan's rulers and, after 1948, with the Jordanians—but Operation Defensive Shield was the upgraded version of this process. The operation's official goal was "to wipe out the Palestinian terror network."[11] Waves of tank and infantry units, supported by Apache

11 These goals were similar to those of Operation Peace for Galilee.

helicopters, rolled into the PNA-controlled West Bank and later Gaza Strip territories, cities, refugee camps, and even villages (leaving only Hebron and Jericho untouched).

The Israeli forces tried to disarm every member of both the official and unofficial militias and to find stores of arms and explosives. They captured and imprisoned thousands of suspects in detention camps. According to Amnesty International, between February 27 and May 20, 2002, 8,500 Palestinians were arrested and held for interrogation. Most were gradually released.[12] But the Israeli forces did not stop here. They systematically destroyed buildings and infrastructure, radio and television stations, databases and documents—some of which were taken to Israel as the spoils of war—thus destroying years of hard work by Palestinians during the post-Oslo period. Water treatment facilities, power-generating plants, and roads were damaged or completely bulldozed. This operation not only destroyed political organizations and their facilities but civilian institutions like universities, schools, clinics, churches, and mosques under the pretext that terrorists were hidden inside.

Regular and irregular Palestinian militias resisted minimally. There was apparently some understanding that Israeli military superiority was so overwhelming that it was unwise to give them a pretext for

12 The 2,000 or so held in administrative detention during February and March were released, but those detained after March 29 were held for a long time under the most difficult conditions. According to a military order issued on April 5, 2002, it was permissible to hold someone under administrative detention for eighteen days without a court order and without contact with a lawyer or family member. After this period, it was possible to request from the courts an extension to ninety days. By the end of May, less than 1,000 men remained in detention, conditions improved, and visits from Red Cross representatives were made possible.

using their full capability and causing even more destruction and human casualties. The only place besides Nablus where fighting broke out between irregular Palestinian forces and the Israeli forces was in the Jenin Refugee Camp.

The Palestinians in Nablus also resisted, but because there were almost no Israeli casualties, the battle over Nablus did not receive much attention. The fighting occurred in the period from April 2 to 21, mostly in the Old City, the Casbah, and the Balata and Asqar Refugee Camps. The Palestinians reported eighty killed and 300 wounded. Nablus is traditionally considered the hub of Palestinian resistance, and the Casbah is viewed as a place foreigners are not allowed to enter.

Even before the Israelis entered the Jenin camp, the various militias like Fatah, Hamas, and Islamic Jihad united in a Jenin Camp General Leadership Command to fortify and booby-trap the camp. Israeli forces trying to penetrate it fell into the trap that had been prepared for them and for three days, between April 2 and April 5, were unable to take over the camp. In response, Israel brought in bull-dozers and overcame resistance by passing from house to house through walls they had knocked down. These tactics resulted in the total destruction of two neighboring camps to the south, Damj and Hawashin.

On April 9, the Israelis requested a ceasefire in order to evacuate eight wounded soldiers and thirteen corpses from a building that had blown up while they were inside. At the end of the hostilities, street warfare, which was greatly feared by both sides, had occurred only in the Jenin Refugee Camp and, to a more limited degree, in downtown Nablus. The result was fifty Palestinian dead, an unknown number injured, and an immense destruction of property which had left about 5,000 people without homes. On the Israeli side, twenty-three soldiers were killed and over 100 injured in the battle for Jenin.

Because the Israelis closed off all access to the region, even for the media and rescue teams, rumors circulated that a massacre was being carried out in the Jenin Camp and that many Palestinian bodies had been buried in a mass grave in the northern Jordan Valley. The rumors proved groundless. Nonetheless, Israel itself admitted that excessive force surpassing international norms had been used in the battle. This included the use of human shields, the taking of hostages, and the denial of aid to the injured, all of which are defined as war crimes. United Nations Secretary General Kofi Annan appointed a committee to investigate the Jenin events, but Israel refused to allow it to enter the area. Whatever happened in Jenin to the Palestinians, the events in the refugee camp took on contradictory meanings: on the one hand, there was a heroic story of Palestinian victory over the powerful Israeli army (like Karameh in 1968); on the other, there was a story of misery and massacre (like Deir Yassin, Kafr Qassem, Sabra and Shatila, or Tal al-Zaatar). Later, a similar but smaller incident happened in Hebron. On the evening of November 16, a small Palestinian unit ambushed an Israeli patrol in Hebron's Jabel Juwarah neighborhood.[13] During four and a half hours of fighting,

13 In the City of Hebron, about 600 Jewish religious zealots live among 160,000 Palestinian inhabitants. These settlers behave like masters of the city, continually harassing the Arabs. An entire Israeli brigade of soldiers guarantees the security of this small handful of settlers. Because the settlement is close to the site known as the Ibrahamia Mosque or the Cave of the Patriarchs (*Machpelah*), a site holy to both Jews and Muslims, the Jewish community of Hebron regularly plays host to thousands of Jews for prayers that are more like political demonstrations. Thus, large numbers of

nine Israeli soldiers were killed, including the Israeli commander of the region, and fourteen soldiers were wounded. Three armed Jewish civilians were also killed, as were three guerilla fighters belonging to the Islamic Jihad.

Two other notable events occurred during Operation Defensive Shield. One was the siege of the Church of the Nativity and the other the siege of Yasser Arafat's headquarters. Immediately upon Israel's entry into Bethlehem in early April, a large group of Palestinian militiamen sought sanctuary in the Church of the Nativity. They assumed, correctly, that Israel would not attack such an important Christian holy place. The whole affair aroused great anger in the Christian world against both Muslims and Jews. It also underscored the unique and sensitive nature of this battle over the Holy Land and the complex relationship between the three religions. When battles erupted around the building itself, the Pope intervened personally along with officials from some of the European states that had promised to grant asylum to the Christian fighters. The affair was concluded within a month.

When Israel first entered Ramallah, the largest, most modern, and most secular of the Palestinian cities, military forces surrounded Arafat's headquarters (the *Muqata*) in the city. Arafat, together with other PNA officers and politicians, was put under virtual house arrest.[14] The siege of the *Muqata* did not end on April 21, when the

the Arab inhabitants of the city are under curfew most of the time. The settler population in Kiryat Arba, a settlement on the eastern flank of Hebron, is about 6,500 inhabitants.

14 At the same time, Fatah Secretary Marwan Barghouti was brought to Israel and put under administrative detention for an extended period. Barghouti was

Israeli forces retreated from other parts of the city, because Israel demanded the extradition of the wanted men holed up in the compound.[15] Throughout the siege, Israeli politicians, various experts, and journalists debated whether Arafat should be killed or deported and whether or not there was a viable replacement for him. During this episode, Arafat was not even permitted to attend the Summit Conference of the Arab states in Beirut. At the conference, it was decided to propose regional peace with Israel in exchange for withdrawal to the 1967 borders, the establishment of a Palestinian state with East Jerusalem as its capital, and a reasonable and agreeable solution to the refugee problem.[16] Israel completely ignored this unprecedented resolution, even as a basis for further negotiations.

The siege ended when American intervention secured Arafat's release and he, in exchange, turned the men wanted by Israel over to the Americans, who imprisoned them in Jericho. This affair will certainly have long-term consequences for Arafat and perhaps for the

---

suspected of being the commander of Fatah's underground arm, the Al-Aqsa Martyrs' Brigade. Later, he was subjected to a political show-trial in Israel. He did not recognize the authority of the Israeli court because he was an elected political leader of another people and he therefore refused to be defended.

15 Among those who sought asylum there were Ahmed Sadat, Secretary of the Popular Front and the man responsible for the execution of the Israeli Minister of Tourism Rehavam Zeevi—the head of the Moledet Party, who explicitly demanded the ethnic cleansing ("transfer") of the Palestinians—and Fuad Shubki, the financier who supposedly organized the voyage of the Karine A, a small ship carrying armaments to the PNA. After long negotiations, the men were transferred to a prison in Jericho under Anglo-American protection.

16 It is possible that Arafat was not interested in going to Beirut both because he feared he would not be allowed to return and because he was uncertain about the Saudi peace proposal, which was the main item on the summit's agenda and which he viewed as an American initiative.

PNA as well. Arafat's agreement to buy his own freedom by handing over others damaged his prestige. The prolonged siege emphasized his weakness and his dependence on Israel, the Americans, and the Europeans. For the first time, PNA members themselves demanded far-reaching governmental and legal reforms. Still, it is unlikely that genuine reforms will be implemented during these especially difficult times, even if Arafat himself espouses them and the Legislative Council adopts them. Other demands for reforms came from both Israel and the US, yet their intentions were diametrically opposed to those of the legislative council. They wanted the removal of Arafat and the construction of a different authority that would suppress Palestinian resistance and comply with long-term interim agreements that were in accordance with Israeli interests.

The general staff of the Israeli armed forces had for four months demanded that the political leadership allow it to regain control over the Palestinian territories, including the Gaza Strip. However, the political window of opportunity for this move seemed closed, mostly because of the international reaction, and on April 21 the operation was officially declared to be over. Later, the reserve forces called up for the occupation of the Gaza Strip were released. The reality was, however, that Israeli forces continued to enter Palestinian cities and refugee camps almost daily in order to arrest and sometimes kill people. Israel continued its policy of besieging the West Bank and dividing it into unconnected parts while the Palestinian groups continued their acts of terror, albeit to a lesser degree, both inside Israel and against the settlements and traffic in the West Bank. Soon, however, the suicide bombings were resumed. In June, Israel launched Operation Determined Path by re-occupying all of Area A for an indefinite period. This inter-communal war, which blurred any differences between front and rear, civilians and military, set off a chain reaction leading to much increased violence. An aspect of such inter-communal wars is that individuals on both sides possess strong personal feelings about the management of the conflict and are deeply involved in it. What also characterizes such conflicts is the disappearance of any empathy for the aspirations, feelings, attitudes, and suffering of the other side.

If the symbol of the first Intifada was Palestinian children throwing stones, the symbol of the al-Aqsa Intifada—for both sides—is the suicide bombers. The reaction of the two groups toward the suicide bombing reflects the inability of each to understand its opponent. The Israeli Jews see the phenomenon as the ultimate proof of the cruel, zealous, and primitive Palestinian nature and conclude that it is impossible to engage in reasonable negotiations with people who send their children to kill both themselves and innocent people. The Israeli media is filled with stories about suicide bombers being regarded as heroes and martyrs while their surviving family members are given both social honor and material compensation. At the same time, Israelis ignore academic work like that done by cultural studies scholar Idit Zertal showing that Israel also has a death ethos, although it is not manifested in suicide bombings.[17] This lack of understanding has blinded most of the Israeli population to the poverty, the life-long

17 The suicide bombers are frequently mocked and their motivations derided by sexual explanations for their actions. They supposedly sacrifice themselves for the seventy virgins that are given to martyrs when they arrive in heaven. The motif does indeed exist in popular Islam, but this explanation is too simplistic and ignores the fact that some bombers are secular or female and the motivation is political (nationalistic, religious, or a mixture of the two).

harassment and humiliation, the hopelessness, and the perpetual violence and killing that blight so many Palestinian lives and lead so many young Palestinians to such desperate acts—acts that are not dissimilar to the one the Bible ascribes to Samson after he was captured by the Philistines. The same lack of empathy has also blinded Palestinians to Jewish grief and anger when suicide bombers massacre innocent civilians, emotions that are intensified when many Palestinians publicly express their happiness after every successful operation. Often the funerals of victims on both sides become wild political demonstrations and rites of hate.

Aside from the curfews, which often last for weeks, and the closures, which partition the territories into small cantons and prevent any freedom of movement for individuals while denying access to food and medical care, the most evil actions from the Palestinian point of view—equivalent in their eyes to the suicide bombings—are the targeted killings. On December 17, 2000, Israel initiated a policy of extra-judicial executions (called targeted killings) of those believed responsible for terrorist acts and armed resistance. Tanzim officer Samih al-Malabi was among the first murdered. While most of those executed were responsible for terrorist acts, others seemed simply to be available members of the Palestinian leadership. Some analysts suspected that the Israeli Government cynically used executions to provoke a Palestinian reaction and forestall any attempt to subdue the violence.[18] There were two reasons why these killings stirred such

18 This seemed to be true of at least some of the executions—e.g., on December 30, 2000, Fatah Secretary General of the West Bank Dr. Thabat Thabat; on January 14, 2001, Raad al-Karmi, the head of the Tanzim in Tulkaram; on April 4, Iyad Khadran, leader of the Islamic Jihad in Jenin; on August 25, Abu Ali Mustafa,

powerful emotions among the Palestinians and some Jews: first of all, the murder victims were public figures, many of whom were admired by the Palestinian people; secondly, the operations were often not clean, and killed other, innocent, individuals along with the targeted person. When Salah Shehada was executed, nine children and eight other adults were slaughtered with him after a one-ton bomb was dropped on a building he was in. Ariel Sharon praised this carefully planned operation as a great success.

Following it, some members of the Israeli public openly labeled such actions war crimes—one of the few times in Israeli history that this has occurred. The Commander of the Israeli air force, General Dan Halutz, responded to the accusation in an interview for *Ha'aretz Magazine*:

Halutz: All those people who talked about a flagrantly illegal order and threatened to hand over the pilots to the court in The Hague have simply gone off the rails, in my opinion. Is this the public for which the Israeli Defense Forces are fighting day in and day out? All those bleeding hearts who have the gall to use Mafioso methods to blackmail fighters—I don't recall that they ever threatened to turn

secretary of the Popular Front; and on July 23, 2002, Salah Shehada, a Hamas activist. Following the last of these executions Akiva Eldar, a very well-informed commentator for *Ha'aretz* wrote: "Since the evidence in this case is classified top secret, there's no way to know whether Israeli intelligence, which knew of every step that Salah Shehada and his guests took, also knew that the Tanzim held a meeting last weekend with Hamas in which they discussed, among other things, sending Shehada away on a very long vacation. In other words, in discussions between EU representatives and Ahmed Yassin [the Hamas spiritual and political leader], the Hamas leader was told that it wouldn't be enough for the political wing of Hamas to join the agreement, the military wing would also have to sign."

over one of the arch-terrorists, the terrorists who have killed many Israeli civilians, to The Hague. What I have to say about those people is that this is a democracy, where everyone can always express his opinion. But not to be a traitor.

Reporter: Are you suggesting that the members of the Gush Shalom [Peace Bloc; a tiny group of radical peace activists] who made those comments should be put on trial for treason?

Halutz: We have to find the right clause in the law and put them on trial in Israel. Yes. You wanted to talk to me about morality, and I say that a state that does not protect itself is acting immorally. A state that does not back up its fighters will not survive. Happily, the State of Israel does back up its fighters. This vocal but negligible minority brings to mind dark times in the history of the Jewish people, when a minority among us went and informed on another part of the nation. That must not happen again. Who would have believed that pilots of the air force would find their cars spray-painted with savage graffiti because of a mission they carried out.[19]

19 Indeed the State's General Attorney was requested to try the Peace Bloc, which called on the military and civilians to collect evidence about war crimes committed by Israeli soldiers in the occupied territories. However, the investigation was soon dropped, probably out of fear of opening a Pandora's Box by re-examining the terms "war crime" and "duty to disobey obviously illegal orders," which were recognized and accepted by the Israeli High Court of Justice in 1957 following the trial of participants in the Kafr Qassem massacre, but have never been used since then. Foreign countries have also looked into the possibility of trying Israeli officials for war crimes. On September 30, 2002, Scotland Yard began investigating Shaul Mofaz because of allegations of war crimes. Mofaz was on a fund-raising visit in Britain, but flew back to Israel after Sharon offered him the post of Minister of

High-ranking officers and officials occupying key positions in Sharon's administration recently expressed opinions that should be interpreted as attempts to prepare the Israeli public for far-reaching measures against the Palestinians.

For example, on August 30, 2002, in one of his first public appearances, the newly appointed Chief of Staff Moshe Ya'alon produced an unforgettable "diagnosis" for *Ha'aretz Magazine* that could have been taken directly from a *Der Stuermer*-style publication:

Ya'alon: The characteristics of the threat [from the Palestinians] are invisible, like cancer. When you are attacked externally, you can see the attack, you are wounded. Cancer, on the other hand, is something internal. Therefore, I find it more disturbing because here the diagnosis is critical . . . I maintain that this is a cancer . . . My professional diagnosis is that this is a phenomenon that constitutes an existential threat.

Reporter: Does this mean that what you are doing now as Chief of Staff in the West Bank and Gaza is applying chemotherapy?

Ya'alon: There are all kinds of solutions to cancerous manifestations. Some will say it is necessary to amputate organs. But at the moment, I am applying chemotherapy. Yes.

Defense. An interesting suit was filed in a Belgian court at the end of 2001 against Ariel Sharon, Rafael Eitan, Amir Drori, and Amos Yaron, the persons found responsible by an Israeli commission for the massacre in Sabra and Shatila, by the victims' families, for war crimes. In June 2002, the court decided that it lacked the authority to try them.

And further echoing Sharon's view, Ya'alon said:

> I have no doubt that when this period will be viewed historically, the
> conclusion will be that the War of Independence has been the most
> important event in our history and the present war was the second
> most important event . . . [because] it brings us back to the pre-state
> [era], the partition proposal and the War of Independence . . . [the
> Palestinians do not want] to reach an agreement and settle their
> claims, but to preserve the conflict and let time run its course
> according to [their] phase strategy [of destroying Israel in stages].

As usual, the reporter avoided asking hard questions, like how the
Palestinians' refusal to accept Barak's "most generous offer" fitted in
with the supposed "stage strategy." The reporter also did not clarify
the meaning of the "invisible threat" and why it is "internal"—when
conventional Israeli wisdom locates the Palestinians of the occupied
territories outside the boundaries of the Israeli state. Is it possible that
Ya'alon was talking also about the Arab citizens of Israel as a cancer,
or perhaps not only about Arabs?

Another highly emotional issue to both parties—but also a tool
used to manipulate local and world opinion—is the intentional or
unintentional killing of children. On October 1, an Amnesty International report condemned both sides in the conflict for their "utter
disregard" for the lives of the 250 Palestinian and 72 Israeli children
killed in the conflict. From the beginning of the al-Aqsa Intifada to
September 2002, more than 625 Israelis were killed in a total of
14,280 attacks in two years. During the same period, some 1,372
Palestinians have been killed by Israeli military forces. A total of

4,500 Israelis were injured in terrorist attacks, and among the Palestinians the numbers are much higher—the Palestinian Red Crescent reported about 20,000 injured.

At the end of Sharon's first term, was he still an enigma or a leader whose intentions had been clearly defined? Was he a de Gaulle or a Milošević? Whatever conclusion one draws on these questions, it is clear that he has achieved one of the major objectives of his first term—to be re-elected and gain another four years in which to implement his ideas.

20   What is Left of the Left?

Before analyzing Sharon's likely intentions and the likelihood of his implementing those intentions—which are not necessarily identical with those of his hard-core constituency[20]—it is essential to understand what happened to the Israeli left, or more specifically, to the peace camp. The peace camp, which developed during the past decade or so and whose views were often expressed at the ballot box, was formed from a shaky coalition of diverse groups with highly different motivations and views.

---

20 A considerable portion of his hard-core constituency did not vote for him during the Likud primaries but for Netanyahu (who tried to make his own comeback by taking a more hard-line position), and in the general elections for the more extreme rightwing National Union or National Religious Party. However, it was highly convenient for Sharon to establish himself as a moderately rightwing candidate. This strategy proved itself during the January 2003 election, when Likud succeeded in capturing a considerable portion of the centrist electorate and in becoming (with thirty-eight seats) the biggest party in Israel.

Barak, Sharon, and religious fundamentalists from both sides did much to shatter this coalition. The hard-core peace camp was composed of individuals and small groups who believed that the occupation and oppression of another people and the theft of their land were evil in universal humanistic terms, while others in the peace camp believed that the occupation transformed the country into a *Herrenvolk* democracy that corrupted Israeli society itself. Most of these ideas began to be formulated and expressed following the 1982 War although they existed in some form before that.

One compelling reason for reaching an agreement with the Palestinians, even if it includes withdrawal from all the occupied territories and the dismantlement of all settlements, is the military reason. A demilitarized Palestinian state cannot pose an existential threat to Israel, but policing a rebellious occupied people poses a long-term threat because the resulting attrition of Israeli forces constitutes a real danger in the event of a regional war. This perception was probably the reason that Yitzhak Rabin initiated the Oslo process and fashioned the Accords the way he did. Recently, the Israeli military historian Martin van Creveld, in an interview on Australian television, expressed it this way: "Basically it's always a question of the relationship [balance] of forces. If you are strong, and you are fighting the weak, you are going to become weak yourself. . . . If you are strong and you are fighting the weak, then anything you do is criminal."

This thinking underlies another approach that is subscribed to by some people sometimes mistakenly identified with the peace camp— the separatist approach. In the same interview van Creveld expressed vividly the separatist ideology:

[The only solution is] building a wall between us and the other side, so tall that even the birds cannot fly over it . . . so as to avoid any kind of friction for a long, long time in the future. . . . Unfortunately, the Israeli army insists against all military logic on being present on both sides of the wall. We could formally finish the problem, at least in Gaza, in forty-eight hours, by getting out and building a proper wall. And then of course, if anybody tries to climb over the wall, we kill him.

Various versions of this idea became very popular among Israeli Jews and the construction of the fence began at the initiative of the former Minister of Defense, Benjamin Ben Eliezer, more or less along the pre-1967 lines. In fact, the fence around the Gaza Strip was completed a long time ago and the Strip has become the largest concentration camp ever to exist. The separatists do not belong to the part of the peace camp that desires peace and co-existence between the Jews and Arabs, even if many of them are identified with the left because they are willing to abandon the settlements, make territorial concessions, and accept the establishment of a Palestinian state in order to get rid of the Palestinians. Some separatists would also support giving up parts of Israeli territory that are densely populated by Arabs. What they desire is the opposite of ethnic cleansing but it would have a similar practical and psychological outcome.[21] It is rooted in a mixture of intertwined emotions: distrust, fear, and a hatred of Arabs combined with the desire to remove Israel from its immediate cultural milieu. This

21 This approach is the settlers' nightmare because it means a complete abandonment not only of the settlements and the settlers, but also of the ideology of Greater Israel. That is the reason that the settlers regard it as the "ethnic cleansing of Jews from their homeland."

explains why the majority of the Israeli population—as consistently shown by all the public opinion polls in recent years—votes for rightwing or religious parties headed by the Likud, favors the elimination of Arafat, and at the same time agrees with the establishment of a Palestinian state. The separatists also opt for establishing national unity governments, hoping that Labor hawks and moderate Likud members will make the Arabs disappear from the Jewish state through a unilateral move. The separatists were only temporary allies of the peace camp, as evidenced by their vote for the hawkish Ehud Barak, and they may go back to the Labor Party if Sharon will not provide security by "building a wall so tall that even the birds cannot fly over it."

A vital component of the peace camp is the Arab Israeli citizens' votes and parties. Any time in the past decade that the left bloc won an election, it was achieved mainly because of the Arab voters, who constitute about 18 percent of the eligible voters. The Arab voters have at least two vested interests in supporting the Jewish left and the peace camp. One is to achieve freedom and self-determination for their Palestinian brethren; the second is their hope that the resolution of the Jewish–Palestinian conflict will improve their status as citizens and will provide them with greater—if not full—equality in the Jewish state. But usually the mainstream left alienates them. Even during Rabin's period, the Arab Israeli parties were not officially part of the coalition and got funds but not positions, a situation that left them feeling like the political equivalent of the other woman. During Barak's term, Arab Israeli citizens were killed during demonstrations. Their justified disappointment with Barak and other partners on the left led large numbers of them to withdraw from politics and had a devastating impact on the peace camp.

However, the major causes of the left's decline were Barak's failure to achieve an agreement at Camp David, his "no partner" declaration, Labor's decision to join the National Unity Government, and the failure of Meretz and its affiliated movement Peace Now to support two grass-roots initiatives that would have broken long-held Israeli conventions about making war and peace.

The first was a movement of regular and reserve soldiers that refused to serve in the occupied territories. Most of these soldiers were not pacifist in the accepted sense of the term (a genuine pacifist movement never existed in Israel). Their refusal is selective; they were ready to be drafted and to be combatant soldiers in unavoidable (so-called no-choice) wars, but refused to participate in smothering the Palestinian revolt, in defending illegal Jewish settlements in the occupied territories, and in committing what they perceived as war crimes or crimes against humanity. All of them were court-martialed and sentenced, often several times, to jail terms of differing lengths under severe conditions.

The father of a young conscientious objector circulated the following message on the Internet:

On Sun, 10 November 2002, Matania Ben-Artzi wrote:
Dear Friends: [My son] Jonathan Ben Artzi finished his fourth term in jail on Friday, Nov.8, 2002. Today, Sunday, Nov. 10, he was called up once again. He asked [the military] for civil service [instead of military service], stating that his beliefs did not allow him to serve in the army. This request was rejected, and he was sentenced to a fifth term in jail, for 28 days.

The Colonel who sentenced him didn't let him talk, but here is what he intended to tell him (and what he has asked me to distribute): "According to an Amnesty International [report], more than fifty children under the age of twelve have been killed by Israeli Army fire during the first seven months of 2002 alone. You have not sentenced even one of the perpetrators of these crimes. But you're sentencing me for the fifth time, just because I refuse take part in such activities."[22]

Here are some excerpts from another famous letter, written to an Israeli general, by Yigal Bronner:

Dear General,

In your letter to me, you wrote that "given the ongoing war in Judea, Samaria [the West Bank] and the Gaza Strip, and in view of the military needs," I am called upon to "participate in army operations." . . . I am writing to tell you that I do not intend to heed your call.

During the 1980s, Ariel Sharon erected dozens of settler colonies in the heart of the occupied territories, a strategy whose ultimate goal was the subjugation of the Palestinian people and the expropriation of their land. Today, these colonies control nearly half of the occupied territories and are strangling Palestinian cities and villages as well as obstructing—if not altogether prohibiting—the movement of their residents. Sharon is now Prime Minister, and in the past year he has been advancing toward the definitive stage of the initiative he began twenty years ago. Indeed, Sharon gave his order to his lackey, the

---

22 Jonathan Ben-Artzi began serving his seventh consecutive prison sentence in January 2003. He has been sentenced to a total of 190 days.

Defense Minister [Benjamin Ben Eliezer], and from there it trickled down the chain of command. . . .

I am [an] artilleryman. I am the small screw in the perfect war machine. I am the last and smallest link in the chain of command. I am supposed to simply follow orders—to reduce my existence down to stimulus and reaction, to hear the sound of "fire" and pull the trigger, to bring the overall plan to completion. And I am supposed to do all this with the simplicity and naturalness of a robot, who—at most—feels the shaking tremor of the tank as the missile is launched towards the target.

But as Bertolt Brecht wrote:

> General, your tank is a powerful vehicle
> It smashes down forests and crushes a hundred men.
> But it has one defect:
> It needs a driver . . .
> General, man is very useful.
> He can fly and he can kill.
> But he has one defect:
> He can think.

And indeed, general . . . I can think. . . . Perhaps I am not capable of much more than that. [But] I can see where you are leading me. I understand that we will kill, destroy, get hurt and die, and that there is no end in sight. I know that the "ongoing war" of which you speak will go on and on. I can see that if "military needs" lead us to lay siege to, hunt down, and starve a whole people, then something about these "needs" is terribly wrong.

I am therefore forced to disobey your call. I will not pull the trigger. . . . So general, before you shoo me away, perhaps you too should begin to think.

Since the beginning of al-Aqsa Intifada, there have been more than 180 draftees who have refused to serve in the occupied territories and many more who have signed oaths to refuse if they are called up. It is a relatively large number but not enough to constitute a critical mass that will undermine the logic and the machinery of occupation. These objectors are organized or supported by small, radical leftist groups.[23] However, the leftist Meretz and its offshoot, the large and well-funded Peace Now movement, have refused to support them, claiming that in a democratic regime, the refusal to serve is not only unlawful but immoral.[24]

Needless to say, this argument is a complete nonsense and unrelated to the Israeli sociopolitical reality. Its definition of Israeli democracy is religiously or nationally defined, encompassing only Jews, and failing to include the millions of other people under Israeli rule or control. Israel long ago ceased to be a democracy when it stopped regarding the occupation as temporary and began incorporating occupied lands into the state while excluding the populations of

23 Examples of such groups are the long-established Yesh Gvul ("There is a Limit," but also "There is a Border"), and the newly formed New Profile and Ha'ometz Lesarev ("The Courage to Refuse").

24 Usually it is complemented by the immortal argument "and what if the soldiers with religious or rightwing beliefs refuse to obey orders to evacuate settlements or to withdraw from occupied territories on the basis of their conscience?"

those lands from any framework that guaranteed their civil and human rights. As was stated earlier, Israel can no longer be considered a liberal democracy, but has become a *Herrenvolk* democracy. Although Israel began a process of democratization after the Oslo Accords, it was halted after Rabin's assassination and the democratic gains made under his rule were gradually dismantled.

Therefore, any non-violent act that aims to end the occupation is undoubtedly a democratic one. What the mainstream left and peace movement failed to realize when they rejected the option of supporting and legitimizing conscientious objection was precisely this cardinal point. Thus, for example, Amnesty International published on December 18, 2002 an address to the Israeli Minister of Defense:

> Members of the IDF [Israeli Defense Forces] who commit grave human rights violations and war crimes, such as killing children and other unarmed civilians, recklessly shooting and shelling densely populated residential areas or blowing up houses on top of people and leaving them to die under the rubble are not brought to justice and held accountable for their acts. . . . At the same time conscripts and reservists who refuse to serve, precisely to avoid participating in such acts, are sent to jail for months. What kind of message is such a policy sending to Israeli society?

The assessment of the above-mentioned pacifist groups was that supporting conscientious objection would greatly increase the phenomenon. It is hard to see how the government, and especially the military, would handle thousands of conscientious objectors and their supportive families.[25] Indeed, this would represent a dramatic shift in the militaristic Israeli culture and would require the type of moral courage and willingness to take political risks that the Israeli left has always lacked. Civil disobedience on such a massive scale would cause a major cleavage within Israeli society; however, without such a break, it is difficult to imagine how the present tragic impasse might be brought to an end.[26] An Israeli intellectual, Tanya Reinhart, estimated that the "ideological peace camp" constitutes about one-third of Israeli citizens, a figure that probably includes Israeli Arab citizens, who are not drafted in any case. Jewish ideological supporters of a complete or nearly complete withdrawal from the territories include about 15 to 20 percent of the Jewish population. This figure does not include separatists, who care neither about peaceful coexis-

25 There is a large but unknown amount of gray draft-refusal. Many would-be draftees avoid presenting their refusal as a moral or ideological statement and ask for exemption from service mainly under the rubric of medical, personal or family hardship. The military is fully aware of this phenomenon and usually grants such exemptions in order not to accentuate the political or moral objections. After all, it would be very embarrassing to the system to imprison thousands of people, most of them from educated and professional middle-class families, for refusal. The relatively light punishment, usually twenty-eight days in jail—sometimes in several terms— and then exemption if the man won't break, reflect the confusion of the military system in dealing with a phenomenon that is unusual in the Israeli cultural landscape. Usually the ideological objectors ask to serve within the Green Line or to do non-military national service (an option open mainly to religious young women), but are refused and brought to court.

26 Usually such a clash of values, in this case between the tribal and civic interpretations of Judaism, cannot be solved without some sort of civil war, but any support of any kind of violence against an unarmed civilian population is basically immoral. However, Israel can't afford a civil war, although it has been involved for a long time in a fierce if not always explicit *kulturkampf*. Massive civil disobedience is the opposite of civil war but will have the same outcome.

tence with the Palestinians nor about the settlements. Although the peace camp is a minority, its weakness lies not in its numbers but in the fact that they are armchair activists. The small minority who are active—like the conscientious objectors—are promptly labeled radical leftists even by their supposedly leftist counterparts. However, if this group became as active as the settlers, who have made considerable personal and collective sacrifices and taken significant risks for their beliefs, the result would be massive civil disobedience that would bring down the entire system of colonization and oppression. The major sin of Meretz as a party and of Yossi Sarid personally is to ignore the objectors who are supported by small, radical groups and thus miss the opportunity for a major breakthrough.

Another smaller but symbolically important opportunity was missed when Meretz and Labor failed to pressure the previous government to ratify the Rome Statute of the International Criminal Court. The treaty that established the ICC was approved by 120 nations, including Russia, France, and Great Britain. The United States, China, Libya, Iraq, Qatar, Yemen, and Israel voted against it. The Rome Statute became effective on July 1, 2002. In order to participate in the nomination and election of judges and prosecutors, states should have completed the ratification process by November 31, 2002. Without ratification the signature is only a declarative act.[27] Although Israel

27 Israel, along with the United States, has long undermined world attempts to establish a criminal court with international jurisdiction. In the ICC discussions in Rome, the United States required, for example, that states or their citizens must consent to their investigation by an ICC prosecutor. Can one imagine what would happen if US law required that criminal suspects consent to their investigation and trial? Israel and the US also feared overzealous and politically biased prosecutors inventing or distorting claims against them. Another objection was that terror was

signed the Rome Statute of the ICC on December 31, 2000, signing an international treaty is only an expression of basic agreement with it. The signatory is not bound by the provisions of the treaty until the state ratifies it, something that Israel has not yet done.

The Rome Statute defines war crimes as grave breaches of the Fourth Geneva Convention, and also defines, *inter alia*, crimes against humanity, crimes against peace, and crimes of aggression. The Statute declares that war crimes are "serious violations of the laws and customs applicable in international armed conflict, within the established framework of international law."[28] The Statute is the culmination of efforts to limit violence in war that began in the

---

not included in the Statute as a war crime, probably because its proper definition is hard and controversial, like the definition of state terrorism. However, many of the articles of the Statute do cover terror-like acts as crimes, even though the term terrorism is not used because of the difficulties in defining it.

28 The list of violations of the rules governing the conduct of war is long, but here is a list of those that seem most relevant to the Israeli–Palestinian conflict: (i) intentionally directing attacks against the civilian population as such or against individual civilians not taking part directly in hostilities; (ii) intentionally directing attacks against civilian objects, that is, objects which are not military objectives; (iii) intentionally directing attacks against personnel, installations, material, units, or vehicles involved in humanitarian assistance or on a peace-keeping mission in accordance with the Charter of the United Nations, as long as they are entitled to the protection given to civilians or civilian objects under the international law of armed conflict; (iv) intentionally launching an attack in the knowledge that such an attack will cause incidental loss of life or injury to civilians or damage to civilian objects or widespread, long-term, and severe damage to the natural environment which would be clearly excessive in relation to the concrete and direct overall military advantage anticipated; (v) attacking or bombarding, by whatever means, towns, villages, dwellings, or buildings which are undefended and which are not military objectives; (viii) the transfer, directly or indirectly, by the occupying power of parts of its own civilian population into the territory it occupies, or the deportation or transfer of all or parts of the population of the occupied territory within or outside this territory.

mid-nineteenth century and were further formalized in multinational meetings and agreements in The Hague in 1899 and 1907. The preamble to the 1907 treaty asserted that both "the inhabitants and the belligerents remain under the protection and the rule of the principles of the law of nations as they result from the usages established among civilized peoples, from the laws of humanity, and the dictates of the public conscience."

A proper opposition movement that is committed to human rights and a universalistic ethic should seize the opportunity provided by the Rome Statute and world interest in it to make the Israeli public, and especially the military, aware of the precise nature of the war crimes being committed.

There are many reasons why making Israeli society aware of these crimes would be a difficult task. Many Jews believe that a Jewish army could never commit such crimes and that war crimes and crimes against humanity are always committed against Jews but almost never by Jews. If the Israeli military does something that is not completely "according to the rules," it is always in the interest of self-defense or some just cause. Others believe, although not necessarily explicitly or consciously, that after so much suffering inflicted on Jews by gentiles, Jews are fully entitled to be cruel or assertive toward non-Jews.[29] An additional factor is the tendency to attribute an almost religious sacredness to the military. This combination of factors leads politicians and political parties to recoil from discussions about the war crimes

29 One of the most abused mechanisms of righteousness is the memory of the Holocaust. A common argument in internal disputes among the Jews themselves when discussing conflict between Jews and non-Jews is "to speak in the name of the Holocaust victims" or survivors.

Israel may have committed, an attitude that is understandable but not justifiable. Thus only a small but vocal group, the Peace Bloc, headed by veteran journalist and uncompromising peace activist Uri Avnery, has tried to draw public attention to the new International Criminal Court and its relevance to the acts of war committed by both sides in the Israeli–Palestinian dispute, and its efforts met with limited success. The Peace Bloc was probably not naive enough to think it would be able to bring Israeli officers and leaders to the ICC (after all, victors are never tried for war crimes), but hoped to raise the issue in the public sphere and perhaps deter some activities against the Palestinians, like the devastation wreaked on the inhabitants of Jenin, extrajudicial executions, mass detentions, or the starvation of the population.

The co-option of the Labor Party during Sharon's first term, the indiscriminate attacks on Israeli civilians in the heartland of the country, and the failure of the Camp David talks led to the fragmentation of the peace camp and the paralysis of most of its members but also to the revitalization and radicalization of small groups and non-governmental humanitarian organizations. It also resulted in the creation of dozens of new groups. Among them is Ta'ayush, an assertive group founded in October 2000 and comprising both Jewish and Arab young people and students who organize humanitarian activities such as providing convoys of supplies for needy Palestinians, but who also organize political protests or participate in those organized by other groups.[30] Peace Now, founded in the late

30 In a recent and amazing Hebrew book *Where Am I in this Story?* the human-rights activist Daphna Golan-Agnon writes about the varied humanitarian, civil-rights,

1970s, has become an umbrella organization for these small groups. It possesses a secretariat and some more or less mainstream intellectual leaders and supporters (like the writers Amos Oz and A.B. Yehoshua) but lacks an up-to-date political agenda (though it has up-to-date slogans). These many small and fragmented groups fill the vacuum left by the leftist parties but are unable to counterbalance the rightwing parties.

21   The Non-Violent Guerilla War

This penultimate chapter is devoted to the reproduction of three reports originating from three different NGOs, along with parts of a study conducted by a team of Palestinian community researchers. The three reports—made by eyewitnesses, each in their unique style—demonstrate that political activity has been reduced to the provision of localized humanitarian aid by Israeli and international groups. These responses to violence can be regarded as a kind of non-violent guerilla warfare against the occupying regime—activities carried out by Israeli Jews, Israeli Palestinians, and others. The researchers' study documents the profound effects the violence generated by the ongoing politicide has had on Palestinian schoolchildren.

The three reports share two things in common: they describe specific activities within the general context of the Israeli–Palestinian

---

and political activities engaged in by herself and others. Dr. Golan-Agmon, who is a lecturer at the Law Faculty of the Hebrew University, also emphasizes the overwhelming number of women in these NGOs.

inter-communal war, and they are powerful, deeply personal eyewit-ness testimonies that display a subtle irony regarding the situation and the actors' own roles in it. The first story is taken from a daily report by members of an NGO called MachsomWatch, a hybrid Hebrew-English word for Checkpoint Watch. Soldiers at these loca-tions are supposed to check every Palestinian wanting to leave occupied territory. The official reason for these checkpoints is to prevent the entrance of terrorists, suicide bombers, and other suspects into Israel. In reality, the checkpoints provide no real security because Palestinians intending to cause harm have 101 alternative ways to enter Israel.[31] The MachsomWatch was established in February 2001 by Jewish and Palestinian female volunteers, who observe these checkpoints in order to prevent the harassment of Palestinians by soldiers. However, frequently the observers themselves are mistreated by soldiers manning the checkpoints. The reports are reproduced with minimal editing in order to preserve their authenticity.

*

Report no. 1
Sunday morning, November 3rd, 2002, at al-Khader roadblocks and girls' secondary school
Team: Chaya O., Lauren E., Maya R.
General: While the week in Israel was marked by the delayed and

31 However, some suicide bombers and other attackers targeted these irritating checkpoints themselves. Some argue that the real reason for the checkpoints is to calm the scared Jewish population by demonstrating that the security forces are protecting them.

much to be celebrated end of the governmental partnership/coalition between Labor and Likud and the rather limited uncertainties regarding what it will all boil down to, the week in Palestine was marked by much of the same in terms of killing, curfews, closures, and arrests. This last item among the atrocities should receive special notice: we should bear in mind that hardly a day passes without the detention and incarceration of Palestinians. On some days, the number of additional prisoners ranges between 3 and 5, on others it rises to several dozen. The current invasion of Jenin, now completing its second week, has alone yielded a "crop" of more than 160 new prisoners. This implies that Israeli detention centers are currently packed with many thousands of Palestinians (I believe the numbers are somewhere between 7,000 and 8,000, though I may be wrong—Maya), the majority of whom were arrested between Operation Defensive Shield and now. Most of these have not been brought to trial while many others were labeled "administrative detainees." Families of the imprisoned are prevented from visiting them; some—mainly families of those who were imprisoned during earlier stages of the Intifada or prior to that (veteran prisoners)—have not visited their sons/brothers/husbands/fathers for more than two years.

House demolitions have now become a daily IDF practice; here, too, it appears that the total of the last few months outnumbers the sum total of houses demolished since the end of the first Intifada. If this pace continues, soon there will not be much left of Jenin. . . .

Hebron has been subjected to four straight days of curfew, that is, before, during and after the commemoration of "Shabbat Chayey Sarah" [the Torah recitation] by settlers and their visitors. The military arrangements taken to enable the successful celebration of the occasion also affected the neighboring Bethlehem district, which witnessed tightened closure and enhanced military presence Thursday through Saturday.

Our shift:
Upon arrival at al-Khader junction and its roadblocks (around 7.20 am) we noticed a "procedure" yet unknown to us: two soldiers (regulars) who were standing in the middle of a large number of Palestinians, who were entering and exiting the roadblocks, ordered these pedestrians to stand in rows while they carried out a (brief) ID check. Some women and elderly people escaped the check and walked around the soldiers, but most "submitted" without question or noticeable signs of resentment. We were told by one Palestinian and later by the soldiers themselves that the "reason" behind this measure was a "warning" [about a possible suicide bomber from the region]. It should be noted that the soldiers were not at all rude and that they did their best not to delay people (it took no more than a few seconds for each to show an ID and move on). Nevertheless the practice, which has now become more and more widespread and established, of enforcing border-checks upon Palestinians who are moving within the (compressed) confines of a single West Bank district, is totally outrageous.

Less than one hundred meters to the east of the junction, at the improvised taxi and minibus station behind the second roadblock, we were soon to enter what began as a heated conversation with several taxi-drivers of the al-Khader–Ramallah–al-Khader route. The situation of these men is so desperate that some were on the verge of exploding when we approached them with a casual "good morning." Their morning, it turned out, was not only bad, it also started at 1 am, when they queued up for the day's shift. By 7.30, without having even started their engines, some of them could have easily burst into tears. At first they yelled at us for practicing human rights "on shifts," that is for not being available when and where we [the watchers] were most needed—or as they put it straightforwardly, in Wad-a-Nar on Saturday mornings and Thursday afternoons. The first is the time when employees and laborers from the southern West Bank head to their workplaces in the Ramallah and Jericho districts, the second is the time of their return home for the week's day off. The army and border police tend to be especially obnoxious on these occasions, stopping taxis for hours (some reported having been made to wait for four and even five hours in the middle of this wasteland through which the Wad-a-Nar route passes). After voicing their complaints about our uselessness, the drivers calmed down and told us their story.

The men we were talking to are part of a group of some fifteen taxi-drivers from the Hebron district. All of them carry pleasant recollections from the pre-September 2000 era, when they used to drive all over the place, covering the routes from south Hebron in the south to Jenin in the north and Allenby Bridge [on the Jordan River, the border between the West and East Bank] in the east, as well as occasionally entering Israel proper. Although the taxes imposed by the PNA at the time were high, according to them they managed to make not less than 8000 shekels [approximately US$1,500] per month. Shortly after the commencement of the Intifada and the enforcement of the full closure policy, as we have reiterated in our reports over and over again, they were no longer permitted to drive on the now "Arab-free" main roads and were forced to confine themselves to the internal (often unpaved) secondary roads, along which, nonetheless, numerous checkpoints, roadblocks, and obstacles are scattered. To cut a two-year-long story short, these fifteen drivers decided to rent a house in al-Khader (near the roadblocks) together. Since the number of passengers who travel outside the district on a daily basis has shrunk to unprecedented levels (as a result of the infinite difficulties encountered on the way, as well as the economic crisis—most people cannot afford to pay the 15 shekel charge for a drive from al-Khader to Ramallah), no more than one drive per day (back and forth) can be guaranteed for each driver. And even this requires queuing beforehand and other pre-arrangements between the drivers to eliminate competition and fighting.

So, just imagine, starting one's day at 1am and waiting, at times for seven, eight or even twelve hours, for one ride, which may last for ever given the Wadi-Nar [the name means a sudden rift in the earth] ordeal. In fact they spend almost their entire day and night around the "station"; it is there where they eat excessively greasy and not very clean falafel, and there where they have a bitter coffee, and there where they stand and chat forever. In the evening they retreat to their rented home from which they re-emerge a few hours later. At the end of each week, they return home to their families for a day off. Yusef, the driver who did most of the talking, is a father of ten from [the village of] Yata. He estimated his entire monthly income after all this hardship as ranging between 1000 [$200] and 1500 shekels [$300] and not exceeding 2000 shekels.

Leaving the taxi-drivers, we headed with heavy hearts toward a girls' secondary school, where we were lucky to be approached by the Headmistress Um-Shadi as soon as we entered the courtyard. Together with her was an elegantly dressed woman, who turned out to be the Ministry of Education's Physical Education Supervisor for the Bethlehem region. Both Headmistress and Supervisor were very eager to speak with us, and Um-Shadi was soon to recount yesterday's (Saturday, November 2) events, which commenced when the army noticed what appeared to them to be a suspicious vehicle, parked near the al-Khader "club" not far from the girls' school, and decided to blow it up without any warning or delay (they did not even try to inquire about the owner). Um-Shadi rushed to calm the girls in advance. However, shortly after the explosives went off, and without any apparent reason, the soldiers began shooting tear gas in the school's vicinity. The wind brought clouds of gas into the courtyard, where girls had just started a sports class, and soon after into the classrooms. Um-Shadi was quick to lock three pregnant teachers in a back room, from which she hurried to take care of the girls, many of whom felt dizzy and in pain. Although she managed to calm everyone down, it was impossible to resume classes in this atmosphere, and Um-Shadi dismissed the girls.

Having recounted these details, Um-Shadi and Rabiha Atallah (the supervisor), now joined also by the sports teacher (Khawla), were happy to move on to relatively more pleasant topics, ranging from gymnastics to the mastery of languages, to the differences between [Shaul] Mofaz [the newly appointed Minister of Defense and the previous Chief of Staff] and [Benjamin] Ben Eliezer. All three are second (or third, in the case of Khawla) generation refugees—Um-Shadi's family originated from Ein-Karem [a western Jerusalem neighborhood], Rabiha's from Zakaria, and Khawla's from Jura (near Moshav Ora)—who are extremely energetic and involved, and all eager for further contact and cooperation.

*

The next report was written by Sylvia Piterman in the form of a letter to her son after she participated in an olive-harvest campaign. The months of October and November are the olive-harvest season. Olives are a major Palestinian crop and form the basis of numerous traditional village industries, which press olive oil and make soap, perfume, and other products. In the autumn of 2002, Jewish settlers decided to demonstrate their title over the land by getting rid of the villagers and harvesting the olives themselves. Several Israeli peace groups, mainly under the guidance of Peace Now activist Yaakov Manor, Peace Bloc activists Adam Keller and Yehudith Harel, and Ta'ayush members, decided to help the Palestinian villagers who had been robbed of their crops.

*

Report no. 2
November 15, 2002
Dear Son,
Yesterday we once again went on an olive-picking mission in the occupied territories, only this time it did involve risking our lives. There were ten of us, Israelis and internationals, plus the driver—a Palestinian from East Jerusalem. It was indeed a tiny group, which was nice since during the last few weeks, the bigger groups I have joined were stopped by the army many times and we arrived very late at the villages. . . . We were heading to Ein Abus, a small village located next to Itzhar—a settlement notorious for the extremism of its inhabitants.

When we arrived at Ein Abus the loudspeaker on the Mosque's

minaret spread the news that a group of peace volunteers was ripe
and ready to tackle the villagers' ripe and ready olives. We were
divided into two groups and headed to different groves. Only a few
Palestinian villagers joined our little group: a middle-aged woman
(mother of twelve children), her elderly mother, a kid riding on a
donkey and another boy. Our driver also joined our group, and he
was the only one among us who spoke both Arabic and Hebrew.

We had walked for about ten minutes when we first saw him, and
it was obviously a settler, standing on the top of the hill. He shouted at
us in Hebrew, demanding that we go back to where we came from.
We continued walking toward the olive grove, and then the settler
started shooting at us. It was pretty scary so we lay close to the ground.
The head of our group—Hillel—used his cell-phone, calling the army,
the police, the radio, and whoever he thought could be of help.

Then the settler seemed to have stopped shooting and we got up.
The Palestinians, upon our request, went to an area that was not
visible from the top of the hill. They gave us the sacks and a big piece
of tarpaulin (or canvas) to be put on the ground, under the trees, to
catch the falling olives, and we continued climbing toward the grove.
Finally we got to the trees and started picking olives.

But after a short while, we realized that about a dozen settlers
were coming toward us from the opposite side of the hill. Once they
were close enough to us, they started shouting at us and shooting in
the air. They cursed us and called us Nazis. We ignored them and
kept on picking olives, while the head of our group was calling the
army and the police, asking for their protection from the settlers.
Then one of the settlers authoritatively demanded to have our ID
cards. We asked him if he had a police ID card, which he—

obviously—did not have. The settler said he would kill us next time we came.

The settlers—shaved heads covered by big skullcaps, and long side-locks around their faces—were obviously maddened by their failure to make us retreat. They tried to scare us, jumping at us and toting their guns. At some point they went down the hill and we were afraid they would attack the Palestinians down the road so two of us went down to warn the villagers, but this was unnecessary. The villagers had already run away.

Finally, the military arrived: three obviously young soldiers. They told us to leave right away as we didn't have a permit from the army to be there. We refused to leave, saying that we did have a permit and we urged them to check this. We continued to pick olives all the time, so the soldiers said that if we didn't leave the place immediately they would call the police and we would all be arrested. We continued to pick olives.

Then the other group of volunteers, headed by Yaakov, one of the leading figures in the olive-harvest campaign, showed up in "our" grove. It turned out that one of them had got hit on the head by a stone thrown at him by a settler and had been taken to the hospital by ambulance. His group decided not to go any further and back-tracked toward us. The truth was that there were not too many olives left in the grove: the settlers had already stripped many trees and taken the olives away. We put the olives that we had picked in several sacks and carried them down the hill toward the village. When we got back to the village, the Palestinians received us very warmly. And even if we couldn't speak with them, body language was enough to tell us that they were friendly toward us.

This morning a group of sixty volunteers returned to Ein Abus, in order to complete the job we couldn't do yesterday. . . . At the grove many IDF soldiers, headed by a reserve captain, joined us. The trees there had few olives left on them. The settlers indeed seemed to have done a pretty thorough job on them. And I couldn't resist asking the captain if, to his mind, it was fair that the villagers could not pick their olives off the trees unless a group of volunteers came to their aid, forcing—that way—the army to shield us from the settlers.

The captain was very friendly, almost charming, and he promised me that had the villagers asked for the army's protection, it would have been provided for them. But they simply didn't ask. Regrettably, there was not a grain of truth in what he told me. The truth is that the army had been in cahoots all along with the settlers, preventing the villagers from getting to their groves, using all sorts of excuses. The captain emphasized that there was a dangerous Hamas group at the village, and that was why the settlers needed guns. Interestingly, the army didn't think that it needed to accompany us, when we went into the village today and the day before, to protect us from that danger.

I also asked the captain what the settlers were doing there. He said that the settler presence in those hills is a political issue that will be decided on January 28 [the election day].[32] Since this captain is one of

32 The writer of this eyewitness account told the author of the present book the following: "On another occasion, the army stopped us and made a scene as if it had found explosives in a car. We waited for more than four hours and we got to the village at 3pm. At that time of the day, you cannot do much. Nevertheless, we, the group from Jerusalem, went to Kafr Yanum and helped a family pick its olives. . . .

Sharon's advisors, it means that if Sharon wins the elections, then Itzhar, Itamar, Tapuach, and Hebron [the most extremist settlements of the West Bank] will not be included in the "painful concessions for peace" [Sharon's expression]. This would mean an era of endless fighting and economic decline.

You know, son, my visits to Ein Abus left me angry and frustrated to no end, and I still do not know what to do with this anger and frustration. Do you have any good advice for me?

Love, Ima

*

In North America, many Protestant Christian groups are identified as unconditional supporters of Israel or even as Christian Zionists. However, other Christians have devoted their life to providing human-itarian aid to the Palestinians. One of these NGOs is the Christian Peacemaker Team, an ecumenical initiative working on peacekeeping missions around the world. CPT is sponsored by Mennonites, the Brethren and Friends' Meetings. One of their reports follows.

*

Report no. 3
Hebron Update, Monday, November 18, 2002
Curfew in entire city [of Hebron]. The team received many phone calls from families without food because of the tight curfew. The team made trips out buy food in places they knew would be open,

---

Those explosives were the most famous explosives 'found' during the Intifada. They were reported on the radio countless times and half a page in *Ha'aretz* was devoted to them" (November 3, 2002).

and then delivered the food, mostly milk and bread, to various families in the area.

Greg Rollins and John Lynes, took a visitor from B'Tselem, the Israeli human rights group, to the Jabel Johar neighborhood to see the site of the November 14 shoot-out. Settlers had set up a few tents in the area and the army had begun to set up walls along the road leading to the site of the shooting. Rollins, Sue Rhodes, and two visitors delivered more food to people's homes. Coming through the checkpoint at Duboyya Street they saw a Palestinian man and his son being detained. Soldiers caught the man as he was taking his son to the doctor. The CPTers pleaded with the soldiers for twenty minutes before the soldiers allowed the man and his son to go home.

Leanne Clausen collected information on eighteen families in Wadi Roos, Beqa'a Valley, and the Jabel Johar neighborhood who have received new home demolition orders. The families who received these orders were not connected to the attack, but are in the path of the proposed "buffer zone" being expanded around Kiryat Arba [a settler town near Hebron]. Rollins accompanied a team friend to retrieve his brother who was stranded at a gas station next to a newly set up Israeli military checkpoint in Hebron. On the way, they heard the curfew lifted for a few hours in parts of H1 [an area supposed to be under Palestinian control, near the Jewish settlement]. Curfew in H2 [the area around the so-called Patriarchs' Cave, under Israeli control] was lifted from 8:30–11:00pm.

The team's translator called and reported that soldiers were entering homes in her neighborhood. One soldier ordered an older woman not to look at him. When she did not obey him, he threw a pair of shoes at her. Clausen stayed on the phone with the translator until Mary Lawrence and Kristen Anderson could reach the house. Clausen heard soldiers verbally and physically assaulting the people inside the house. Soldiers left the house shortly after Lawrence and Anderson arrived.

Many families and two of the team's translators told CPT that the Hebron Municipality usually delivers emergency food during curfew, but that the Israeli military has forbidden them to do this, threatening to shoot them if they try.[33] CPT offered to accompany the workers on the delivery if the workers were willing to try going out.

Around 5:00pm, a [Palestinian] family living near Kiryat Arba called the team in a state of panic, saying that settlers had surrounded their house and were stoning it. (The family feared for their lives.) Lawrence, Mary Yoder, Rhodes, Anderson, Lynes, and Jerry Levin went quickly to the house. Clausen and Christine Caton both called the Kiryat Arba police, who hung up on them each time. Clausen then called some Israeli friends of the team who contacted the police on the family's behalf. When the CPTers arrived at the house, they observed a circle of military jeeps in front of the house, and settlers standing off to the side. The family told them that soldiers had quelled the attack, but that the settlers were likely to begin again once the soldiers left. The CPTers decided to spend the night with the family.

At 9:30pm Rollins and a team translator went to Salaam Street to pick up her nephew. On the way back they found vegetables in the

33 Occupation forces must guarantee occupied populations access to food, medical aid, and humanitarian aid under the Fourth Geneva Convention.

Bab Zaweyya, which the team translator took for Palestinian families in the Old City.

Wednesday, November 20, 2002

Curfew in entire city. Lawrence, Yoder, and Rhodes continued food distribution in the Old City and H2 area of Hebron. Rollins met a group from the World Council of Churches Ecumenical Accompaniment Program, who came to visit the team for the day. At 11:00am, Anderson, Caton, Levin, and Lynes responded to a call about a pending home demolition in the al-Manara area of Hebron. Clausen contacted the Israeli Committee Against House Demolitions, who stated that the Israeli High Court [of Justice] had granted permission for demolition of militants' homes. The Israeli military blew up the upper level of the house where one of the shooters from November 15 had lived with his family. The family had been expecting this to happen and had removed their belongings from the house. The soldiers then blew up the house a second time to make sure the upper level was totally destroyed.

Thursday, November 21, 2002

Curfew in entire city. Levin, Rollins, Rhodes, and Lynes, along with members of Israeli Committee Against House Demolitions (ICAHD), went to spend the night with Palestinians in Jabel Johar. Israeli soldiers had already knocked down one house's kitchen wall with a bulldozer, and said the entire house would be demolished in the morning. Soldiers ordered Levin, Lynes, and Katherine Maycock, and Jeff Halper from ICAHD to leave, promising that they would protect the house from settlers. The group was able to spend the night in two other Palestinian homes. No settler incidents noted.

Friday, November 22, 2002

Curfew in entire city. An Israeli lawyer for ICAHD obtained an injunction postponing the demolition of the house the Israeli Army threatened to destroy. Clausen and Anderson delivered food to the Jabel Johar area. En route, they discovered Israeli soldiers detaining some twenty Palestinian men outside a mosque. Neighbors told them the men had been standing there a long time. The CPTers passed by, greeting the soldiers and detained men. After delivering the food they observed all but three men were let go. The CPTers stayed in the area until the three were released and the soldiers left. Anderson, Rhodes, Levin, and Yoder slept in homes along with the Israeli group. The CPTers observed the Israeli soldiers appeared to keep the settlers under control.

*

Finally, this last part of the chapter reproduces a fragment of a study conducted by a team of community fieldworkers affiliated with Bir Zeit University who conducted a series of surveys about the effects of the various Israeli incursions on community life and social services.[34] A portion of their report describes the effects on schooling:

> The past academic year [2001–2002] was particularly traumatic as spiraling poverty gripped the [Palestinian] nation, and as environmental and infrastructural destruction, residential and institutional demo-

---

34 The team comprised Rita Giacaman, Anita Abdullah, Rula Abu Safieh, and Luna Shamieh, who also wrote the reports. The fragments are quoted from a report titled "Schooling at Gunpoint: Palestinian Children's Learning Environment in War-like Conditions," dated December 1, 2002.

lition, death, injury, disability, and the arrest of loved ones as well as the Israeli military re-occupation of the entire West Bank became the new and ongoing way of life. The school system was not spared this destruction. By the end of the 2001–2002 school year, the Ministry of Education reported that 216 students were killed, 2,514 injured, and 164 arrested, 17 teachers and staff in the education sector were killed and 71 were arrested, 1,289 schools were closed for at least three consecutive weeks during the Israeli invasion between March 29 and the end of the school year. Approximately 50 percent of school children and 35,000 employees in the education sector were prevented from reaching their schools. Scores of teachers and students were unable to commute between the rural villages and the urban centers before and after the invasion.

High-school final-year *tawjihi* [baccalaureate] students suffered particular difficulties during the whole year of preparation, and the scheduled examinations were disrupted by military operations and postponed for over a month. Most of these children, especially in the northern West Bank, spent their extended two-to-three-month "summer break" imprisoned at home under strict military curfews and external closures. Many neighborhoods, especially densely populated urban centers, refugee camps, and poor villages, suffered recurrent military incursions, bombardments, extra-judicial executions, combined with the indiscriminate killing and injury of civilians (nearly half of them children), as well as nightly intrusions of soldiers into private homes, arrests, and the brutalization of family members. There has been a continuous destruction of homes, agriculture, and other private and public property like shops, offices, workshops, and service institutions.

The section then concludes:

> As this school survey demonstrates, the ramifications of the Israeli onslaught of the past academic year on schoolchildren surpass the effects of the infrastructural damage to their habitat, both at school and at home, and have had a deep negative influence on children's ability to learn, their sense of security, their mental health, their dignity, and indeed, their consciousness. These children have been violated in every way, and are growing up being dominated by a sense of hate, a sense that can only predispose them to what is called "a tendency toward violent behavior." Indeed, violent behavior is not a genetic predisposition, but is socially constructed. In the Palestinian case, the construction of violence begins and ends with Israeli military occupation.

CONCLUSION: POLITICIDE IN PROGRESS

The first chapter of this book described the continuing crisis that has been an inherent feature of the Israeli state since 1967 and the logical and ideological contradictions of the Israeli right wing. The only logical solutions to this crisis and paradox—the desire to possess the whole Land of Israel without the Palestinian inhabitants who endanger the Jewish character of the state—are to get rid of its unwanted population or alternatively to withdraw to the 1967 border, and perhaps even relinquish part of the lower Galilee, which has a large Arab population. In other words, a partial or complete ethnic cleansing is the one unequivocal answer to the unbearable dissonance existing in rightwing ideology between the desired and the existing realities. The other possible solution acceptable to most Israeli Jews under certain circumstances is a far-reaching territorial compromise. The crisis is rooted in the fact that the Israeli political and cultural system is able neither to conduct a large-scale ethnic cleansing of the area nor negotiate a real compromise acceptable to most of the Palestinians.

Although current political and moral constraints will not allow ethnic cleansing at present, several factors have made it more likely at some time in the future. The Israeli public now—in contrast with the not-so-distant past—considers the Palestinian population's "transfer," the Hebrew euphemism for ethnic cleansing, to be a legitimate subject of discussion.[1] For example, Rabbi Benny Elon, now Minister of Transportation, representing the National Union Party (which has eight seats in the Knesset), has repeatedly expressed the opinion that transfer is not only a viable option and a necessary condition for the survival of the Jewish state but also a humane one, because repatriation to Arab lands spares Palestinians the misery of living under Jewish rule or being killed in military actions.

Ariel Sharon has surrounded himself with officials and advisors who seemingly share these extremist views, like the Minister of Defense, Shaul Mofaz, and Chief of Staff Moshe Ya'alon.[2] Thus, the possibility

1 Rumors about detailed plans for ethnic cleansing have been spread during the past year by the Israeli right wing. Moreover, Palestinians and some Israeli intellectuals have warned of the possibility. One example was an interview given by Benny Elon to the rightwing weekly *Makor Rishon*, in which he discussed secret talks between the US and Israel concerning the re-settlement of hundreds of thousands of Palestinians in Iraq, as a part of the envisioned new order in the Middle East imposed following the US invasion of Iraq. In general, the enthusiastic support by Israel for the Bush administration's campaign against Iraq was viewed in the context of a regional war, with Israeli leaders believing that the war would distract the world's media and allow them to handle Palestinian issues more easily and to employ more drastic measures.

2 During their overlapping terms—Mofaz as Chief of Staff and Sharon as Prime Minister—Mofaz complained many times, even in public, that the PM didn't allow the military free rein to crush the Palestinians and get rid of Arafat. Once, when Mofaz didn't execute a Cabinet decision, Sharon erupted angrily, telling Mofaz

that Ariel Sharon is preparing a grand design, as he did in 1982, or perhaps several, cannot be excluded. His plan would not only include drastic measures to crush the Palestinian armed struggle and prevent terrorist attacks, but would resolve, once and for all, the basic contradiction inherent in the rightwing and religious fundamentalist ideologies by realising their dream of purging the Arabs from the "Land of Israel." After all, Israel, in its short history, has already established a precedent for ethnic cleansing.

Efraim Halevy, Ariel Sharon's close aide, the former head of Mossad, and presently the head of the Israeli National Security Council, said during the above-mentioned Herzliya conference that the rules of engagement would be changed because the *threat* of "mega-terror" acts against Israel can be construed as an attempt to commit genocide against the Israeli people and undermine the very foundation and existence of the state.[3] If the Palestinians continue with their terrorist activities, he added, there is a real possibility that the Palestinian national movement will be eliminated. In such a case, the world will understand and support the Israeli measures. Halevy did not explain what these measures would be.

"There is a Government in Jerusalem." The disagreements between the two men made it surprising that, after Benjamin Ben Eliezer left the National Unity Government, Sharon appointed Mofaz as his replacement. Some analysts concluded that Sharon needed to prevent Mofaz from joining a radical party like the National Union.

3 "Mega-terror" usually refers to an act that may cause many thousands of casualties and a massive destruction of property and infrastructure, most probably by an attack with biological or chemical weapons, but it could also be a spectacular attack like the unsuccessful attempt to hit an Israeli airliner in Kenya with a ground-to-air missile. At the beginning of 2002, it was reported that an attempt at mega-terror was thwarted when security officials detected an explosive device attached to

The possibility of implementing even more extreme measures against the Palestinians has been greatly increased by one of Sharon's most impressive achievements—the link he has forged between the local Palestinian struggle for self-determination, which has used terror, and the American mobilization against world terrorism. Exploiting the tragedy of September 11, Sharon rushed to declare, "Arafat is Bin Laden." Israeli analysts and experts saw this comparison as ridiculous and harmful, but the subsequent adoption of the comparison by both the Bush administration and the American public once again demonstrated Sharon's superior political instincts. This gave him free rein to re-occupy most Palestinian cities and refugee camps and, de facto, to undermine the internal and external legitimacy of the Palestinian authority and to destroy its material and human infrastructure as well.

There can be no doubt that the primary duty of every state is to protect its civilian citizens by all legitimate means, including the use of military force. From this point of view, the Israeli military operations could be considered completely justified and justifiable—if their objectives were limited to deterring further attacks against the Israeli civilian population and eliminating terrorists and terrorist groups. However, this reasoning seems somehow misleading and out of context because it fails to consider the violence inherent in occupying a territory and oppressing its people for decades. The argument that the re-occupation of Palestinian territories was intended solely to protect Israeli citizens from terrorist acts strongly resembled

---

a tanker that was about to enter an oil storage facility in a densely populated region of central Israel.

the declared objectives of Operation Peace for Galilee, because the real aims of both operations contradicted the legitimate goal of securing the safety of the state's citizens. The real goals of the re-occupation are revealed in the *modus operandi* of the various security agencies, whose actions were explicitly designed to irritate the Palestinians and exacerbate their hatred and desire for revenge. These policies can only produce more terror and violence, especially since the Palestinians have not been given any reason to hope for a swift and reasonable settlement. This has created a chain reaction of violence that has had its most significant effects on the Palestinian community. Those outside the Israeli Government, including Israeli civilians and the Jewish community in the US, have been largely indifferent to this state of affairs because the painful losses suffered by Jews and the resultant grief and mourning have destroyed any empathy they might have felt for the personal and collective tragedies, the economic privation, the violence and destruction, suffered by the Palestinians.

The present essay does not pretend to predict the future or guess Sharon's real intentions or plans. However, an attentive reading of his own words, an analysis of recent military operations, and an examination of the present sociopolitical culture in Israel and abroad are enough to conclude that Israel is at present pursuing the gradual and incremental politicide of the Palestinian people. This is a long-term process, often conducted by trial and error, which explores and exploits the diverse opportunities offered by the domestic and international arenas and by the Palestinians themselves.[4]

---

4 Azmi Bishara, one of most prominent Israeli Palestinian intellectuals, complained on September 3, 2002 about the lack of a strategy of liberation: "Many of

The ability to carry out this program of politicide partially depends on the United States. Although the Israeli right has always suspected the US of being pro-Arab because of its oil interests, Israeli liberals and leftists have perceived America as a kind of political and moral superego and believe that what America allows is not only politically possible but also meets a higher standard of morality, as that nation is a symbol of the free world and the ultimate model of democracy and bastion of civil liberties.

However, since September 11, the anti-Arab and anti-Islamic torrents sweeping across America and the increasing political power of the Christian Zionists have created a political climate in which the US Government will not prevent Israel from doing anything it wants to the Palestinians, while also providing it with international legitimacy and protection.[5]

Indeed, one of the earliest of George W. Bush's pronouncements

---

today's operations are motivated by revenge or anger and are not the product of any strategy. When the subject of the presence or absence of a Palestinian strategy is discussed, impatient questioners seek to boil the matter down to whether you are for or against suicide operations. The reduction of national strategy to this question exemplifies the extreme poverty of Palestinian politics in these difficult times, which is also quite tragic." Bishara called for an intra-Palestinian dialogue about the goals and the means of the struggle and clearly opted for a popular Intifada (instead of the armed struggle).

5 According to Protestant fundamentalist theology, the return of Jesus and a happy conclusion to history depend on the Jews returning to the Holy Land and regaining control over Jerusalem. This explains the fundamentalists' unwavering support for Israel. This theology also teaches that the Jews will convert en masse to Christianity, a situation that will effectively bring about the cultural destruction of the Jewish people. The Jewish right wing knows this yet warmly welcomes the fundamentalists' political support, believing that what happens at the end of days is irrelevant to the current political situation.

on the conflict was heartening to the non-fundamentalist Israeli right wing. On June 24, 2002, Bush set forth his proposal for the establishment of a Palestinian state. He did not specify a time for its establishment or suggest borders but required the cessation of all terror or resistance activities and a change in the present Palestinian leadership, a demand that was widely understood to mean that the Palestinians must get rid of Arafat and his loyalists and institute democratic reforms within the PNA. Before the announcement, Arafat's power and prestige had hit rock bottom and Palestinian intellectuals demanded reform and democratization of the regime, but Bush's declaration silenced the internal Palestinian democratic opposition. At a time when the US was waging war in Afghanistan and engaging in warmongering against Iraq, a demand for democratization became synonymous with a demand for obedience to Washington and its definition of democracy, a demand naturally rejected unanimously by Palestinians whatever their evaluation of Arafat's regime. However, at the end of that year, the presidential vision was supplemented by the so-called "road map", which called for the establishment of a state within temporary borders by the end of 2003 (later freezing the finalization of the plan till the Israeli election and the formation of a new government), followed by the withdrawal of Israeli forces from the PNA territories and the holding of elections for a new Palestinian Council there. The Palestinian state within provisional borders will then begin negotiations with Israel on a permanent agreement to be reached by 2005. According to the road map, Israel and the Palestinians will begin formulating a new security cooperation plan only in the second stage, probably when the war with Iraq will have ended. Israel will be required to end the curfews and sieges and cease operating in populated areas. The so-called Quartet of the US, the EU, Russia, and the United Nations will supervise the implementation of the plan. Although the plan calls for the establishment of a vague entity called a Palestinian state, no additional proposals were made, leaving all the matters in dispute—like borders, refugees, and the status of Jerusalem—open. This strategy fits in with Sharon's tactic of buying time to continue his policy of politicide against the Palestinians, a tactic that rests on the assumption that Palestinian irritation will lead to continued terrorist attacks and a corresponding mighty Israeli military response and so forth.

How effective Sharon's tactics are on both sides can be seen in a public opinion poll conducted in early December 2002. More than seven in ten Palestinians and Israelis indicated that they were ready to accept a settlement process based on the Palestinians refraining from violence and the Israelis agreeing to a Palestinian state based on the 1967 borders. Less than one in five Palestinians and Israelis (in both cases the percentages were remarkably similar) were committed to the idea of regaining historical Palestine or holding on to the occupied territories. However, a major proportion of both the Palestinian and Israeli majorities expressed no confidence in the readiness of the other side to give up violence or make the necessary concessions. Thus, a majority of Palestinians have continued to support the use of violent methods in the Intifada while a majority of Israelis continue to favor a violent crackdown by the Israeli military.

Being a person who is able to read maps well, Ariel Sharon found Bush's road map highly convenient. Speaking at the annual meeting of the newspaper editors' committee on November 5, 2002, and on

the same day at the Herzliya Interdisciplinary Center, Sharon expressed
a clear vision of how the conflict should be managed. He said that
with the implementation of the road map proposed by President
Bush, Israel would create a contiguous area of territory in the West
Bank, allowing Palestinians to travel from Jenin to Hebron without
passing through any Israeli roadblocks or checkpoints. This could be
accomplished with a combination of tunnels and bridges. He later
said, however, that Israel would take measures such as "creating
territorial continuity between Palestinian population centers"—i.e.,
withdrawing from cities such as Jenin, Nablus, and Hebron—only
while the Palestinians were still engaged in making a "sincere and
real effort to stop terror." After the required reforms in the Palestinian
Authority have been completed, Sharon said, the next phase of the
Bush plan comes into effect: the establishment of a Palestinian state.

The intention is obvious. The Palestinian state will be formed by
three enclaves around the cities of Jenin, Nablus, and Hebron that
lack territorial contiguity. The plan to connect the enclaves with
tunnels and bridges means that there will be a strong Israeli presence
in most other areas of the West Bank. By comparison, the Bantustans
provided by the Afrikaners for the black population look like symbols
of freedom, sovereignty, and self-determination.

In order to make his intentions clear, Sharon added: "This Palestinian state will be completely demilitarized. It will be allowed to
maintain lightly armed police and internal forces to ensure civil order.
Israel will continue to control all movement in and out of the
Palestinian state, will command its airspace, and not allow it to form
alliances with Israel's enemies." Sharon knows very well that no
Palestinian leader will agree to end the conflict in exchange for a state

with such limited sovereignty; but the very mention of the words "Palestinian state"—a taboo term in the rightwing lexicon—grants him an image of moderation in the international community and a place in the center of the domestic spectrum.[6] However, these moderate gestures buy him an almost unlimited amount of time to continue his process of politicide.

As this essay argues, politicide is a multilevel process, not necessarily anchored to a coherent socio-military doctrine. It is a general approach, with many of the decisions being made in the field, but whose cumulative effects are twofold. The first is the destruction of the Palestinian public sphere, including its leadership and social and material infrastructure. The second effect is to make everyday life for

---

6 Sharon was heavily attacked by his own camp's supporters (like Benjamin Netanyahu and Uzi Landau), but mainly by radical and religious right wingers and settlers' leaders, for his apparent acceptance of a Palestinian state. For example, a certain Dovid Ben Chaim circulated the following hate-mail on the Internet: "(Please forward far and wide) Ariel Sharon: The Manchurian Candidate. How do you like your hemlock? One lump or two? Let's be very clear about this: Generalissimos Sharon and Mitzna have identical visions for Israel. Clearing out "the settlers" and carving out a PLO state within Israel. Period. Now is the time for all good men (ladies, too) to get the heck out of LIKUD and join up on the right. Leave its dead carcass to the maggots of the Left. [Moshe] Arens [a former Minister of Defense] went quietly. You other guys make some noise!! You got a month and a half to pull it together. If it doesn't work, after that, you've got all the time in the world to make the Revolution! For six weeks put everything you've got into it. Find a leader (or two) even if he's not Thomas Jefferson. [Avigdor] Lieberman [head of a Russian faction of the National Union Party] and [Effi] Eitam [leader of the NRP] come to mind. Remember to get to the bottom of things, they say, "follow the money." So who profits from Israeli cynicisms? Arafat, the generalisimo and the Left. UNITE THE RIGHT! Blessed are You, G-d, who gives Your People Israel a mighty arm and the will to use it. Be strong! Be strong! May we all be strengthened! WE ARE TAKING IT ALL BACK AND KEEPING IT!" [Capitalized in original]. The violent style is not exceptional but very frequent among the Jewish religious fundamentalists.

the Palestinians increasingly unbearable by destroying the private sphere and any possibility of normalcy and stability. Creating a famine is another way to create such an effect. Thus, in mid-November, 2002, Israeli forces completely destroyed a three-storey warehouse in Beit Lahiya, a town in the northern Gaza Strip, which had enough flour, cooking oil, and rice to feed 38,000 people for a month. The food belonged to the UN-affiliated World Food Program. Before this, as the Intifada progressed, Israel banned most Palestinian workers from entering Israel, cutting off the main source of income for the densely populated, impoverished Gaza Strip, leaving the UN with the responsibility of feeding, at a minimal level, the Palestinians there.[7] A UN official said in August 2002 that about half of the 3.3 million Palestinians are receiving food aid, a fivefold increase since the violence erupted.

All of these conditions are, according to Sharon, designed to lower Palestinian expectations, crush their resistance, isolate them, make them submit to any arrangement suggested by the Israelis, and eventually cause their "voluntary" mass emigration from the land. Sharon is pragmatic and aware that international opinion will not accept either large-scale ethnic cleansing or the transformation of the Hashemite Kingdom of Jordan into a Palestinian state, as envisioned in his initial program. However, he is carefully observing the international political scene in order to exploit the different

7 On the night of October 12, 2002, five Palestinian workers were killed while they tried to sneak into Israel from the Gaza Strip, near the Karni crossing (in the center of the Strip), in a desperate attempt to find work. An Israeli tank spotted them and fired a shell that killed the five men, none of whom were armed, immediately. They were not suicide bombers, but suicide workers.

situations that will arise. He seeks to weaken not only Palestinian society but also the Israeli opposition, because his war against the Palestinians is intermingled with an internal *Kulturkampf* against some of the factions shaping the character and identity of the Israeli state.

Another battle in this war is the one being waged for world public opinion, especially that of the North American Jewish communities. Even before the attacks on September 11, 2001, the Americans—in contrast with the Europeans—were strongly and stereotypically anti-Arab and anti-Muslim, an attitude that influences their views on the Israel–Palestine conflict. The majority of the American public and mass media gave almost unconditional support to Israel without distinguishing between Israel and the policies of its government. Although many American Jews are unaffiliated with Jewish organizations and hold relatively moderate views on the Israel–Palestine conflict, political activists within the organized Jewish community are often especially vociferous in their anti-Arab views, as are some marginal and conservative academics.

After September 11, the fierceness, irrationality, and frequency of these anti-Arab sentiments increased dramatically. Naturally, this discontentment is thoroughly exploited by the Israelis so that they can intensify their oppression of the Palestinians. However, Israeli policy has provoked heavy criticism from European intellectuals and a few dissident voices in North America. Regrettably, this criticism is often rejected, unexamined, as anti-Semitic. The accusation of anti-Semitism has become a powerful tool for silencing opposition to Israel's oppressive policies. No doubt some old and new anti-Semitic elements in Europe, North and South America, and the Arab world have been emboldened by the criticism of Israel's policies. This phenomenon should be denounced and dealt with using the proper social and legal tools, as should any manifestation of racism. The bona fide moral critics should be very careful with whom and how they ally themselves, but the leaders of Israel have to be aware of their partial responsibility in the awaking of this anti-Semitism.

The strength of anti-Arab sentiments in the US is illustrated by the observations of the political geographer, Professor Oren Yiftachel, of Ben-Gurion University, who also works as a peace and reconciliation activist, in his account of a three-week lecture tour of major American campuses made with Palestinian Professor Rema Hammami of Bir Zeit University. He told the *Boston Globe* that a major shift appears to be taking place in the American debate about the Israel–Palestine conflict—the fading-away of Palestine. He was attacked with dubious facts and supposed evidence that had disappeared from Israeli discourse some time ago, and which demonstrated not just ignorance but the lack of any willingness to listen to counter arguments. Statements like "Jordan is the Palestinian state;" "the Land of Israel was given to the Jews [by God?] and only the Jews;" "Is there even such a thing as a Palestinian people?;" "Jerusalem is not even mentioned in the Koran," were typical.

> The reaction of the audiences was quite similar in most campuses. . . . The discourse was highly polarized and this was most evident in the unwillingness to even listen to a joint Palestinian–Israeli narrative. At almost every campus, audience members arose and exclaimed angrily: "How is it possible that you are not arguing with one another?" "We were cheated: they promised a debate and we got a monologue."

"The American audiences were more interested in dwelling on swastikas on the wall of a public library than in the brutal occupation of Palestine, the on-going Israeli violation of international laws and norms, and the mass killing of innocent Palestinian and Israeli civilians"—added Yiftachel wryly.

Regardless of what the attitudes of North Americans and Europeans are, the fate of the Israeli state and of the Palestinian people will be decided on the ground in the Middle East. The hard facts are that a Palestinian people exists, no matter how "old" it is, and that the possibility of their politicide—or their being ethnically cleansed from the country—without a fatal outcome for Israel is nil. The Palestinian people, like many other peoples organized in sovereign states, are basically a creation of a colonial world-system, even if their social and political development was hampered by the same colonial Empire (the British) and by the Jewish colonization of Palestine (which also began under the British colonial umbrella, without whose existence the emergence of a Jewish state in the region would have been impossible). However, even before the beginning of the contemporary Jewish colonization of Palestine, in 1882, the country was populated by approximately 600,000 Arabs and 20,000 Jews.[8]

On the other hand, Israel is not only an established fact in the region, but also a military, economic, and technological superpower.[9] The Israeli state, like many other immigrant-settler societies, was

8 For a detailed account of Palestinian history, see my book, co-authored with Joel S. Migdal, *The Palestinian People: A History* (Harvard University Press, 2003).

9 The military superiority of Israel is used domestically in both directions: some argue that a military power like Israel does not have to make any concessions to the Arabs, while others argue that a strong country can afford to make such concessions.

born in sin, on the ruins of another culture, one which suffered politicide and a partial ethnic cleansing, even though the new state did not succeed in annihilating the rival aboriginal culture as many other immigrant-settler societies have done. In 1948, it lacked the power to do so and the global post-colonial culture was already unwilling to accept such actions. Unlike Algeria, Zambia, or the Afrikaner state of South Africa, the Palestinians and the other Arab states were unable to get rid of their colonizers. The Jewish state in the Middle East proved its viability against all odds and developed a rich, flourishing, and vital society. All it needed was acceptance as a legitimate entity in the region. Its internal normalcy and continuous development depend, in the long run, on being recognized by the other peoples of the region. This process began with the peace accord signed with Egypt, which can be considered the second biggest victory of Zionism. The biggest victory was the Oslo Accords, despite all their drawbacks, because the Zionist movement's primary victim and adversary recognized the right of a Jewish state to exist in Palestine. This revolutionary change in mainstream Palestinian political thought was, like the Egyptian peace agreement with Israel, a delayed result of the 1967 and 1973 wars.

But the 1967 War had additional and contradictory outcomes that created a continuing crisis in Israeli society. Sharon and his ideology are a manifestation of the crisis that has been building since the beginning of the occupation and Israel's transformation into a *Herren-volk* democracy. What most exemplifies this distorted regime is the fact that when 520 Jews in Hebron celebrate Jewish holidays and receive guests who come to show their solidarity, 160,000 Palestinians in the Old City of Hebron are imprisoned while the settlers use the religious holidays to demonstrate their lordship. All of this occurs with the collusion of thousands of military personnel and hundreds of armed settlers.

Soldiers bursting into private homes, most commonly at night, has become a common occurrence. These raids are carried out under the pretext of searching for terrorists or weapons and are sometimes accompanied by plunder and more often by arbitrary killings. These abuses have been recorded by dozens of eyewitness reports collected by B'Tselem and other human-rights organizations. Even if such events are not ordered from above, the military authorities—in contrast to the conventions of previous periods—do not usually investigate and do not prosecute deviant and even criminal acts, thus signaling to the soldiers that the property, privacy, and even the lives of the Palestinian population are considered of no importance.[10]

The crisis is at its deepest right now. Appropriate leadership is lacking, and the actual or potential leadership that exists on both sides is frightening. Nonetheless, we are closer than ever before to a breakthrough because both parties are beginning to understand that they are in a no-win situation and that no military or political strategy—or combination of the two—will make the opponent

10 Occupation, as a social system, is harmful not only to the occupied but also to the occupier. In early November 2002, under the headline "What have I done?!—a hundred soldiers treated for 'Intifada Syndrome'," *Ma'ariv* reported that a special "rehabilitation village" has been set up to care for former combat soldiers who suffer from deep mental crises, a hundred of whom are at present undergoing treatment. Some suffer from nightmares, and are unable to face up to operational failures and having harmed civilians. Veterans of elite units are being treated at the "Izun" ["Balance"] rehabilitation village near Caesarea, by a staff including seven reserve officers. Orit Mofaz, wife of the new Defense Minister, supports the project. The ex-soldiers' parents finance the treatment.

disappear. Neither the Jews nor the Palestinians will be moved from that piece of land without great harm befalling the other side also. If the hostilities persist, the situation may lead to long-term mutual attrition, resulting in the destruction and disappearance of both societies if the conflict escalates into a regional war, whether non-conventional weapons are used or not. A new Palestinian *Nakba* ("Catastrophe") would be accompanied by a new Jewish Holocaust if the Israeli Jews and the Palestinians fail to conclude that their fates are intertwined, that their interests are mostly mutual and not mutually exclusive. If both sides will make or remake the painful compromises they find unthinkable at present, but which are needed to effect a mutual reconciliation, and will adopt basic humanistic values, they may not only cease being enemies but may find that their common interests lead them to become close allies as well. Without a reconciliation between the Israelis and the Palestinians, the contemporary Jewish state will become a mere footnote in world history.

RECOMMENDED READING

Uri Ben-Eliezer, *The Making of Israeli Militarism*, Bloomington: Indiana University Press, 1998.

Uzi Benziman, *Sharon: An Israeli Caesar*, New York: Adama Books, 1985.

Nachman Ben-Yehuda, *Sacrificing the Truth: Archeology and Myth of Masada*. New York: Humanity Books, 2002.

Robert Fisk, *Pity the Nation: Lebanon at War*, New York: Simon and Schuster, 1990.

Menachem Hofnung, *Democracy, Law and National Security in Israel*, New York: Dartmouth Publishers, 1996.

Baruch Kimmerling, *The Invention and Decline of Israeliness: State, Culture and Military in Israel*, Los Angeles and Berkeley: University of California Press, 2001.

Baruch Kimmerling and Joel S. Migdal, *The Palestinian People: A History*, Cambridge, MA: Harvard University Press, 2003.

Rashid Khalidi, *Under Siege: PLO Decision Making During the 1982 War*, New York: Columbia University Press, 1985.

Ian Lustick, *For the Land and the Lord: Jewish Fundamentalism in Israel*, New York: Council of Foreign Relations, 1988.

—— *Unsettled States / Disputed Lands: Britain and Ireland, France and Algeria, Israel and the West Bank–Gaza*, Ithaca and London: Cornell University Press, 1993.

David Kretzmer, *The Occupation of Justice: The Supreme Court of Israel and the Occupied Territories*, Albany: State University of New York Press, 2002.

Menachem Klein, *The Jerusalem Problem: The Struggle for Permanent Status*, Tampa: University Press of Florida, 2003.

Benny Morris, *The Birth of the Palestinian Refugee Problem, 1947–1949*, Cambridge: Cambridge University Press, 1988.

—— *Israel's Border War 1949–1956: Arab Infiltrators, Israeli Retaliation, and the Countdown to the Suez War*, Oxford and New York: Oxford University Press, 1993.

Laurence J. Silberstein, *The Postzionism Debates: Knowledge and Power in Israeli Culture*, New York: Routledge, 1999.

Ze'ev Schiff and Ehud Ya'ari, *Israel's Lebanon War*, New York: Simon and Schuster, 1985.

Gershon Shafir, *Land, Labour and the Origins of the Israeli–Palestinian Conflict*, Cambridge and New York: Cambridge University Press, 1989.

Avi Shlaim, *War and Peace in the Middle East: A Concise History*, New York: Penguin, 1995.

Ariel Sharon (with David Chanoff), *Warrior: An Autobiography*, New York: Simon and Schuster, 1989.

Ehud Sprinzak, *The Ascendance of Israel's Radical Right*, New York: Oxford University Press, 1991.

Mark Tessler, *A History of the Israeli–Palestinian Conflict*, Bloomington and Indianapolis: Indiana University Press, 1994.

Meira Weiss, *The Chosen Body*, Stanford, CA: Stanford University Press, 2002.

Yael Zerubavel, *Recovered Roots: Collective Memory and the Making of Israeli National Tradition*, Chicago: University of Chicago Press, 1995.

INDEX